Strategic Communication, Corporatism, and Eternal Crisis

This book traces a century of militarised communication that began in the United States in April, 1917, with the institution of the Committee on Public Information (CPI), headed by George Creel and tasked with persuading a divided US public to enter World War I. Creel achieved an historic feat of communication: a nationalising mass mediation event well before any instantaneous mass media technologies were available. The CPI's techniques and strategies have underpinned marketing, public relations, and public diplomacy practices ever since. The book argues that the CPI's influence extends unbroken into the present day, as it provided the communicative and attitudinal bases for a new form of political economy, a form of corporatism, that would come to its fullest flower in the "globalisation" project of the mid-1990s.

Phil Graham is Professor in the Creative Industries Faculty at Queensland University of Technology, Australia

Routledge Focus on Public Relations

1 **Transparency, Public Relations and the Mass Media**
   Combating the Hidden Influences in News Coverage Worldwide
   Katerina Tsetsura and Dean Kruckeberg

2 **Strategic Communication, Corporatism, and Eternal Crisis**
   The Creel Century
   Phil Graham

Strategic Communication, Corporatism, and Eternal Crisis

The Creel Century

Phil Graham

Routledge
Taylor & Francis Group

LONDON AND NEW YORK

First published 2017 by Routledge

2 Park Square, Milton Park, Abingdon, Oxfordshire OX14 4RN
52 Vanderbilt Avenue, New York, NY 10017

Routledge is an imprint of the Taylor & Francis Group, an informa business

First issued in paperback 2020

Library of Congress Cataloging-in-Publication Data
A catalog record for this book has been requested

ISBN: 978-1-138-63629-3 (hbk)
ISBN: 978-0-367-60738-8 (pbk)

Typeset in Times New Roman
by Apex CoVantage, LLC

For Gregory A. Hoyle, the last American Progressive

Contents

Preface   viii

1   Introduction   1

2   National Disunity in an Age of New Human Sciences   14

3   Theorising the CPI   28

4   Globalising Technique   47

5   Neofeudal Corporatism and Its Discontents   65

6   The Military Entertainment Complex: Then and Now   79

7   As We Disappear . . .   95

References   108
Index   122

Preface

I have been thinking and writing about most of the themes in this book for at least 17 years. As circumstance would have it, I ended up writing it to coincide with the 100th anniversary of the Creel Committee. It turned out vastly different than I could have imagined. A few things intervened to change the direction of the manuscript. First was the election of Donald Trump to president of the United States. Second was my surprise encounter with Walter Lippmann, whose dazzling intellect left me gobsmacked and wondering how his work had been relegated to obscurity when it was clearly the foundation for a vast majority of contemporary media and communication theory in the United States and elsewhere. The third was a realisation that the pragmatic theory of fact that Peirce, James, Dewey, and their intellectual heirs developed was in fact rhetoric by a different name. Lippmann provided a corrective by upending Peirce, but it came too late to avoid a century of pragmatic scientism. Lippmann's contribution to the theory of pragmatic perception was ignored until Sue Curry Jansen saw what he had done during her 2012 work. I arrived at similar conclusions independently to her, and my slant on his contributions is slightly different. Jonathan Auerbach's *Weapons of Democracy* also stopped me in my tracks. I think it is probably the best history of the CPI available and is especially insightful in understanding Walter Lippmann's role in shaping progressive America, both before and after the CPI. He has done immeasurably important work in setting the record straight on the role of Ivy Lee and Carl Byoir.

I am grateful to Professor Auerbach for his generous conversation and encouragements during the writing of this piece, and his helpful comments on an earlier draft. I thank and acknowledge Queensland University of Technology who gave me the time to write this. To my old friend and colleague, Allan Luke, with whom I wrote some earlier pieces on some of the themes here, I owe the deepest gratitude for long hours of discussion and endless encouragement. And always to my wife, Dr Naomi Sunderland, whose brilliance keeps me warm, steers me straight, and keeps me sane.

—Espiritu Santo, February 6, 2017

1 Introduction

This book describes the development of what has come to be called "strategic communication," a catch-all term for persuasive communication on the part of military, corporate, and government organisations. The promotional patterns of strategic communication are evident almost everywhere, in the efforts of economists, scientists, and academics of all kinds; to those of journalists, business people, and politicians; to the millions of individuals trying every day to make a "name" for themselves as social media or blogosphere "stars". Those patterns have their roots in one of the most extraordinary efforts of persuasion in human history by what became known as the Creel Committee, the official name of which was the Committee on Public Information (CPI).

The CPI was established on April 14, 1917 by President Woodrow Wilson. Its aim was to garner public support for United States involvement in WWI. That was no small challenge given that Wilson had been re-elected by a slim margin on an anti-war, neutrality platform the previous year. Wilson's slogan was "He kept us out of war". The United States was a mere 50 years out of its own Civil War, the war most destructive of human life in history up to WWI. There were no instantaneous mass media. The CPI did its work in a mostly mechanical, print-based media environment which was highly personal and localised. The results it achieved were nothing short of extraordinary. The sheer quantity of activity the CPI organised is remarkable. In 18 months, the committee generated 75 million copies of commissioned booklets; 1,438 drawings for posters and cards, including the famous Uncle Sam "I Want You" poster by James Montgomery Flagg; more than 40 movies, including *Pershing's Crusaders*, *America's Answer*, and *Under Four Flags*; over 200,000 stereopticon slides; 100,000 copies of its own newspaper every day of the campaign; 755,190 speeches by Creel's Four Minute Men; and 700 photographs per day of military activities. The whole campaign cost $4,912,553 to reach a cumulative audience of over 300 million, again, without any instantaneous mass media (Creel, 1920, Ch. 2).

The CPI's efforts were conducted amidst a throng of newly emerging "human" sciences, with Scientific Management (Taylor, 1911), Scientific Administration (Wilson, 1887), and Scientific Education (Dewey, 1903) beginning to take their place as technocratic forces. Taken together, they comprised a powerful array of new techniques aimed at shaping people's actions, attitudes, and opinions in the context of quickly massifying and urbanising societies. They were to be greatly augmented by the CPI's mass marketing of the war effort. And while the term "marketing" also first appears at the turn of the 20th century (Killebrew and Myrick, 1897), it had to wait for the CPI to make the raw power of its rhetorical potential recognisable once raised to an industrial scale.

In the face of a fractious polity, Wilson's Secretary of War, Newton D. Baker, put the immediate challenge like this:

> Wars are sometimes fought for land, sometimes for dynastic aspiration, and sometimes for ideas and ideals. We were fighting for ideas and ideals, and somebody who realized that, and knew it, had to say it and keep on saying it until it was believed.
>
> (1918, cited in Creel, 1920, p. xv)

Baker's 'somebody' was George Creel, a former "muckraking" ("investigative" in today's terms) journalist, publisher, and police commissioner. He was the architect of a communication program designed to 'weld the people of the United States into one white-hot mass instinct with fraternity, devotion, courage, and deathless determination' (Creel, 1920, p. 5). His task was to talk the country into war. He therefore also had to talk it into unity, into a shared national identity, and into shared national principles. In almost every respect, the CPI's work was the making of modern America, including its symbols, attitudes, and orientations. In aid of the committee's work, there were high levels of literacy, with a mere 6 per cent illiteracy among all people above age 14 by 1910 (National Centre for Education Statistics, 2016).

My main argument in this book is that the CPI's work is central to the development of our current political and economic circumstances. I contend that those circumstances are best understood as neofeudal corporatism and reject the idea that understanding the system as capitalist can lead to useful analysis. I use the term "neofeudal" to highlight the militarism upon which contemporary corporatism depends. In Chapter 5, I elaborate the concept of neofeudal corporatism in more detail, but for the moment, in summary, I define it as a system of political and economic relationships that are militarised, depersonalised, based in systems of extreme delegation, and motivated by an eternal sense of crisis.

From Creel to the time of writing this book runs a century-long arc that proceeds through the sudden integration of a formerly fragmented nation, to the heights of national mass mediations in the 1970s and 1980s, to the globalisation policies of the late 1990s following a "democratised" internet and a failed Eastern Bloc, to a state of rapid civic disintegration still accelerating in early 2017. The methods and strategies that Creel brought to bear upon the people of the United States have since been codified and systematised in various approaches to marketing, public relations, organisational communication, advertising, and public diplomacy that can be traced to post hoc scientistic analysis of the CPI's activities.

The techniques developed by the CPI set the course for mass mediated nationalism. They became greatly amplified once applied through instantaneous mass media technologies, beginning with radio. Like most other techniques, they begin in rarefied, privileged realms, with plant and equipment, legalistic, labour, and skill demands that restrict the techniques to large-scale commercial or governmental entities. Today, though, anybody with access to a digital phone or a computer can become a "broadcaster" of influence, produce broadcast quality recordings and videos, reach an audience of billions, and conduct market research in almost any part of the world, all from the comfort of a lounge room, café, or library. The implications of a global internet connecting 3.5 billion people in a hypercompetitive, ideologically fragmented, and hostile cultural environment, each armed in different degree with a militaristically derived set of techniques, and the production and distribution technologies to match, bear serious consideration. Given what Creel achieved, and what the world now faces by way of organised and random violence, the current cultural disintegration takes on a different hue. No more can we believe the childish admonition that comes with the "sticks and stones" doggerel. Words can kill. Language is material action, capable of quantitative and qualitative effects upon people, cultures, and nations.

We continue to feel the effects of the CPI's efforts today, perhaps more obviously than at any time since it was disbanded in 1919. As we become more obsessed with problems of information, facts, and knowledge, the problems of action, and therefore of ethics, get carelessly backgrounded as mere derivative issues, or as issues beyond the realm of the rational and objective problem-solving techniques that the scientific mindset is restricted to addressing. It may well be that our collective dedication to the 'scientistic' mindset has brought us to the brink of a new world war. The method of the book addresses those problems directly. It synthesises elements of a discourse historical approach (Wodak, 2001) and Kenneth Burke's (1966) 'dramatistic' analysis of language as symbolic action, with a particular emphasis on his rhetoric (1950/1969). It is designed to show up the rhetorical patterns that begin with Creel and continue through to Donald Trump, Brexit, the 2016 repeal of Smith-Mundt Act outlawing propaganda against American people by its own government, and the many 'digital wildfires' of 'post-fact society' (Pomerantsev, 2016). The word dramatistic means a focus on action and ethics, on the "do/do-nots" and "thou shalt nots" of language. It marks a contrast with the scientistic approach concerned with truth, facts, information, and the "is/is-nots" of language (Burke, 1966, pp. 38–39). That is not to suggest that facts and truth do not matter, but simply that a dramatistic approach prioritises action and thus considers facts only in so far as they change what people do.

The term "fact" here and throughout the book refers to truth claims and not truth *per se*. Facts are called 'propositions' in linguistics (Halliday, 1994). They have a distinct grammatical form and are distinguished by being testable in terms of truth. Propositions stand in distinction to the dramatistic categories of language that linguistics calls 'proposals' (Halliday, 1994). Proposals are not testable by truth and quite often take the form of commands, exhortations, or judgements, such as "Get out!", "You probably shouldn't be eating that", or "That was the wrong thing to do". Proposals can be evaluated along many lines, all of them socially and culturally grounded, most often through the semantics of obligation, desirability, and appropriateness (Graham, 2006). I hope to make clear as I proceed that the dramatistic is the most important yet least interrogated aspect of language, while the scientistic is necessarily secondary, both in importance and historically. Yet, as demonstrated by early reactions to the Trump presidency, issues of fact take up much of the oxygen where critical discussions of propaganda, media discourse, and communication are concerned.

Our ongoing failure to comprehend the dramatistic aspects of human communication now threatens our existence. However, the same accidents of history and technology that have brought us once again to the brink of self-destruction may also offer an historic opportunity to better comprehend how we might live together, engage in shared action, and learn to educate in a spirit that moderates ambition, competition, and the violent clatter of hubris-driven personal and cultural hostilities of every kind. A century after Creel, we have as much to learn from his unifying efforts as we do from his militarising motives, both being obverse aspects of the same task. A central thread of my argument is that we are suffering from the long-term effects of rhetoric being misrecognised and misunderstood as a primary, fundamental, and inseparable element of all human communication. We have in fact misunderstood rhetoric as pragmatic social science.

One of the most widely cited pieces in almost every influential social approach to the study of language is Malinowski's (1923) *Supplement I* to Ogden and Richards' *The Meaning of Meaning* (1923/1989, pp. 296–396). It takes a central theoretical place in the work of scholars as diverse as M.A.K. Halliday (1994), Walter Ong (1971), James Carey (1989), Umberto Eco (1989), Jay Lemke (1995), and Kenneth Burke (1950/1969), among many others. The piece is most famous for the 'context of situation' concept, a rearticulation of the notion that the meaning of words depends on many non-verbal factors involved in *where, when, how,* and *by whom* they are said (1923, p. 306). It has proven an invaluable concept for both scientistic and dramatistic analyses of communication. But I think Malinowski's piece offers an even richer vein to pursue in respect of problems that beset the contemporary situation. It can be found in his discussion of a child's language acquisition:

> [A] child's action on the surrounding world is done through the parents, on whom the child acts again by its appeal, mainly its verbal appeal. When the child clamours for a person, it calls and he appears before it. When it wants food or an object or when it wishes some uncomfortable thing or arrangement to be removed, its only means of action is to clamour. . . . To the child, words are therefore . . . efficient modes of action.
>
> (1923, p. 320)

The astonishingly simple and unarguable observation is that, at least for most of us, our first actions upon the world are achieved through others by verbal means. The observation has far-reaching implications. It says that our first interactions are rhetorical, however primitive the rhetoric, because they are acts of persuasion that rely on moving our auditors to action. It is a commonplace of communication theory to recognise a persuasive element in any and all communication—that in communicating, one cannot fail to persuade. But Malinowski here draws our attention to the likelihood that rhetoric is in fact primary and precedes all other linguistic functions, that our first lessons in language are lessons in rhetoric aimed at moving others to action on our behalf, that language is our first means of acting upon the world, and that we first learn to act on the world through others. It also foregrounds a relatively underplayed, yet primary motivating tension between control and dependence in respect of relationships between individuals and their social scene.

To attribute infants with rhetorical skills is to somewhat stretch the concept. Yet it is entirely faithful to its social functions. Kenneth Burke's (1950/1962) rhetoric is helpful in understanding how such tensions play out in ulterior terms as shapers of political economy. Burke bases his rhetoric on the concept of identification. He argues that from Aristotle to Augustine, all the major principles of rhetoric can be understood through the lens of identification. Whether we understand rhetoric to comprise appeals to logic, emotion, common sense, faith, nationality, reputation, religion, or anything else, if we are to persuade, we must first engage our audience in some act of identification. He summarises his position like this: 'You persuade a man [*sic*] only insofar as you can talk his language by speech, gesture, tonality, order, image, attitude, *identifying* your way with his' (1950/1969, p. 59). When we identify with others, we do so under different 'headings', whether they be "nationality", "musical genre", "the New York Mets", "conservative politics", "feminism", "profession", "class", "opinion", or whatever transcendent term allows diverse individuals to share in some form of partisan 'consubstantiality' (p. 21). The paradox is that when we unite along terministic lines of identification, we also engage in division, separating ourselves from others, sometimes to the point of outright hostility, persecution, and in the most extreme cases, mass murder.

Creel's rhetoric had two primary identifications to achieve at a national level. The first was for people to identify as Americans. The second was for them to identify with the view that America should join a distant war against Germany. We will see the particularities associated with achieving those identifications in Chapter 3. At this point, though, the main thing to note is that the techniques Creel deployed were aimed at the level of the nation. The arc I trace here is about how those techniques have been bureaucratised, institutionalised, and "democratised" such that the social basis and function of rhetoric has been lost in a flood of departmentalised or "disciplinary" terms. Rhetoric to sell goods and ideas has been departmentalised as Advertising. Rhetoric to shape public opinion has been departmentalised as Public Relations (PR). Rhetoric designed to achieve political ends has been renamed public diplomacy or political communication. Rhetoric for the management of corporate behaviour is called management or organisational communication. Rhetoric for military ends is called information warfare or psychological operations. Rhetoric for international relations is called Public Diplomacy. The organs of the Entertainment Industries deploy a multitude of rhetorical forms designed to delight, engage, transform, and inform. There is even rhetoric for teaching (not to be confused with rhetoric *about* teaching).

Any student of rhetoric will notice that all those functions are named throughout the history of rhetorical theory as various "offices" (social duties, functions, and services) of rhetoric. Having been broken up and hived off into various academic "disciplines" during the 20th century, their rhetorical roots are today almost entirely obscured. That is especially evident in efforts to theorise 'strategic communication' (Hallahan, Holtzhausen, van Ruler, Verčič, and Sriramesh, 2007). Its definition as 'the purposeful use of communication by an organization to fulfil its mission' is sufficiently broad to include any and all of the functions above and, in surveying the history and constitution of strategic communication, Hallahan et al. (2007) include all of them, with only a passing reference to rhetoric as a sub-discipline informing Organisational Communication and some 'rhetorical schools' of PR. The relatively recent attempts to reintegrate the departmentalised aspects of rhetoric have followed a path through Integrated Marketing Communication (IMC) into strategic communication after the disintegration of mass media audiences and the failure of advertising revenues during the 1990s. That fracturing moment is most often slated to developments in communication technology, which is no doubt true to some significant extent. However, there is just as convincing an argument to understand the fracturing of audiences as a function of rhetorical techniques being addressed to ever-smaller groups of people under the heading of "market segmentation". Such moves have advanced to the point at which a new online publication feels it expedient to launch under the following legend: 'From cabbie to QC: We're not journalists, we're you. Your curated city of opinions, brands and culture' (The Big Smoke, 2016). The ostensive "audience of one" has become a norm, as evidenced by iTunes, YouTube, MeVo, MySchool, Me Bank, and the innumerable brand names beginning with some permutation of personal pronoun or possessive adjectival, beginning with the iPod and MySpace.

When we foreground the dramatistic aspect of what has come to be called strategic communication, what we notice throughout the history that Creel set in motion is the social and cultural violence of the CPI's techniques. Over the past century, that violence has been "democratised", diffused, along with scientist command of its techniques, both through education systems and through sheer osmosis in the presence of overwhelming amounts of industrialised rhetoric. The implications and effects of such an environment are everywhere in evidence. The notion of "sending a message" has taken on the most sinister tones. As I write, the outgoing vice president of the United States has declared his intention to 'send a message' to Russia over bombings in Syria by launching a cyberattack against the country (Robertson, 2017). Russia has sent its own message in return by moving its nuclear arms towards the Polish border. This in the same week as the United States accuses Russia of 'posturing to the rest of the world by prepping civilians for potential war, instructing them to check on the availability of bomb shelters and gas masks' (Robertson, 2017).

In India, we see the apotheosis of aggressive corporate pedagogy in the awkwardly named Amity College of Corporate Warfare, which is run by a retired Major General and which offers an MBA in Competitive Intelligence and Corporate Warfare (Amity Education, 2016). In an apparent irony, the eligibility to undertake the MBA includes having an 'amicable personality' and being 'creative with exceptionally high level of soft skills' (2016). Those attributes are entirely consistent when seen through the lens of the Creel century. Writing for *Psychology Today*, Judith Sills (2008) advises the ambitious individual that 'just north of your reputation and east of your resume is yet another man-made mountain to which you might aspire. It's your Brand, the identifying marks of You, Inc., and it can be created as consciously as Disney's Matterhorn'. Tom Peters (1997) is credited with having launched the idea of the personal brand with *The Brand Called You*, although its general thrust can be traced back to Carnegie's (1937) *How To Win Friends and Influence People*. The leading admonition in all such tracts, from Carnegie onwards, is "stand out from the crowd" by which is meant "elicit identification with success" or, in common parlance, "beat the others to the buck".

Rhetoric assumes conflict. In most cases, it is conflict. In all cases, it assumes what Burke calls 'the Scramble, the Wrangle of the Market Place, the flurries and flare-ups of the Human Barnyard, the Give and Take, the wavering line of pressure and counterpressure, . . . the onus of ownership, the War of Nerves, the War' (1950/1969, p. 50). He refers to systemic encouragements to continual bids for higher status, more power, more wide-spread recognition, more money, more fulsome praise, more everything. The long arc of industrialised rhetoric applied at national and international levels runs directly from Creel's "Brand America" to "Brand You". At the same time, the character of that arc as rhetoric has become hidden, even from most experts in the field of strategic communication, the institutional home of rhetoric by another name. Such a situation is ideal for the flourishing of neofeudal corporatism, with the original tensions between dependence and control that Malinowski points to with his parable of the rhetorical infant being amplified through the medium of entire social systems given over to militarised rhetoric in search of both personal and corporate profit.

What This Book Does and Does Not

My aim here is to trace the historical diffusion of persuasive techniques developed by the CPI a century ago and elaborate the implications of that diffusion to help understand today's political economy. Technique is a troublesome term. I mean it here as shorthand for how we do things, or "ways of doing". Techniques are means rather than ends, although one could be forgiven for confusing the two in today's environment. So, I am tracing a century of relationships between industrialised rhetorical techniques and social environments. Or, how the deployment and diffusion of rhetorical technique has redounded against political economic formations over the last century. And while I am concerned with language and linguistic forms and am using elements of a discourse historical approach, especially in situating the CPI in a discursive background of scientistic pragmatism, I am not doing close text-analytic work as might be expected given some of my other work in these areas (e.g., Graham, 2006, 2016). Because of the constraints of space here, I must also limit the degree to which I discuss other approaches to issues either central or peripheral to this book. There are many ways the centennial of the Creel Committee might be discussed: as the apex, decline, and resurgence of mass mediated nationalism; as prefiguring the trans-formation of media technologies; as an exercise in political economy of communication; as political communication; as the birth of "the military entertainment complex"; as the production and exchange of social or cul-tural capital on national levels; as the cradle of the media monopoly system; or as the first public pedagogies of the era of industrialised nationalism. Then there is the mass of business-oriented literature on advertising, mar-keting, PR, branding theory, and the many disciplinary terms that I have already gathered under the heading of "strategic communication". I direct the interested reader to earlier works of mine and others that address those areas in varying degree and have listed the most relevant of them in note 1.[1]

Perhaps the main objection to be raised against the approach I am taking lies in the reversal of a typical relationship between context and technique. In other language, I am risking a kind of "technological determinism" by attributing to technique an agentive role, a role as "grammatical" subject in political economic change. For Burke, it would be more typically the case that the character of the context (or 'Scene') would shape 'means-selection' (1935/1984, p. 113; 1945/1962). For example, an "emergency" situation would call for "emergency" measures (1961, p. 188). But I am arguing that, because they are also forms of action (rhetoric), the particular sets of techniques Creel deployed reverse the relationships such that "emergency" measures can be made to call for "emergency" situations. Or to put the inversion in clichéd form as an economist-pundit recently did (apparently by accident) while discussing a surprise interest rate cut by the Austral-ian Reserve Bank: 'desperate measures call for desperate times' (Charlton, 2016). Because they are rhetorical, the techniques I am describing can bring situations into being. They are forms of action on the surrounding socius: appeals for action, exhortations to opinion, and above all, calls for identifi-cation and the kinds of acts that flow from identification.

My argument may thus far suggest an attack on rhetoric. The opposite is the case. I might as well launch an attack on daylight. I am arguing that rhetoric is an unavoidable and primary fact of human interaction and that we should recognise it for what it is, especially given that there is well over 2,000 years of excellent scholarship on its various guises and func-tions. Walter Ong was clear on the significance of rhetoric being fractured and dispersed. He says that 'the displacement and rearrangement of rhetoric is, from one point of view, the story of the modern world' (1971, p. 8). But rhetoric became 'a bad word for those given to technology because it represented "soft" thinking' (p. 8). It became a bad word for 'those given to romanticism because it seemed to hint that the controlling element was a contrivance' as opposed to the freedom of 'spontaneous' expression to which romanticism aspires (p. 8). Overall, he argues, rhetoric was the last remnant of the oral mindset, that like other functional remnants of the oral, its functions were hived off into various departments, increasingly 'visualised', and that its operation became 'more indirect' as a result. Thus, he concludes, the 'history of rhetoric simply mirrors the evolution of society' (p. 9). I am arguing the opposite: that changes in society, at least over the last century, are best understood as a function of changes in a broken and hidden rhetoric, the power of which has gone widely misunderstood and misrecognised. There have been numerous attempts throughout the century to repair the damage in critical studies of propaganda, literacy, media, culture, philosophy, language, and discourse. However, I argue here that until we understand 'its co-extension with language', our rhetoric and its effects on the social system will remain beyond our control (p. 9).

Plan for the Rest of the Book

Chapter 2 outlines the intellectual and cultural environment into which the Creel Committee was introduced. At the same time as control of people started getting scientific, immigration to the United States was exploding. Between 1900 and 1914, Ellis Island processed between 5,000 and 10,000 people every day, with over a million immigrants passing through it in 1907 alone. In his 1914 declaration of neutrality, Wilson noted the simmering intercultural tensions throughout the United States and the possible impacts the war could have upon them. His fears were well founded. Creel would have to work with the social divisions of a neutrality that had frustrated the various tribes of European immigrants in the United States. Key among Creel's challenges was that promoting the cause of war also entailed talking into existence a unified nation. The deep divisions in the country, along with increasing waves of immigration, undoubtedly gave impetus to a nationalising impulse for Wilson. For Creel, that boiled down to a massive sales job.

Chapter 3 sets the activities of the CPI within a theoretical framework. It outlines the technical and cultural systems within which the CPI operated, how it activated those systems, and how its success is best understood theoretically in order to make sense of current circumstances. The chapter presents theory that combines political economy of communication, Burke's dramatism, and social theories of meaning, including Cooley (1909) and Bourdieu (1998), to argue for a perspective that accepts reality for a social level of cognition. The arc of scientifically organised mass public opinion really begins with Creel and, despite the many criticisms that

Walter Lippmann and others have made about his errors, boosterisms, and omissions (Auerbach, 2015; Jansen, 2012; Lippmann, 1922), in the spirit of dialectical enquiry, I take Creel's 1920 account of what the CPI did at face value. There is no indication that Creel had anything other than sheer instinct and a feeling for public opinion gained through his experience as a journalist to inform the ways in which the CPI achieved what it did, and his response to the challenge can be read as a response to the milieu of the era.

Chapter 4 gives an historical perspective on the propagation of the CPI's techniques. Post hoc theorisations of the CPI's efforts really begin with Lippmann, whose influence on all communication scholarship to follow is incalculable (Jansen, 2012; Auerbach, 2015). The success of the CPI led to its activities being studied with great intensity up to the beginning of WWII. Reactions were as mixed as they were divisive. For the most part, those studies have led to increasingly scientistic, quantitative, behaviourist, and visual approaches. The 'entertainmentisation' that occurred as a function of those analyses is closely tied to a systematic disregard for the dramatistic, ethical, and rhetorical aspects of human relatedness (Postman, 1985). The CPI's activities led to the development of what is now called strategic communication. Its theory and practice are taught in business schools all over the world, and many components are even taught in high schools. Their militaristic roots, though, are almost never taught alongside their theory and practice. The implications of those trends in a political economy characterised by a Hobbesian "war of all against all", and with the means for every person with access to a computer and internet connection to engage in personalised forms of warfare, have wide-ranging implications that are only just beginning to be felt in full.

Chapter 5 articulates a view of current circumstances as "neofeudal corporatism". It connects that view to the history of strategic communication in Chapter 4. I use the reference to "neofeudalism" as planned anachronism to foreground the fact that a new set of aggressive social relations based on constant threats has come to dominate national political economies rather than to argue there has been a return to any previous system. There are similarities though, between current and mediaeval forms, especially where the *comitatus* relationship is concerned. The comitatus was a group of warriors whose organisation was based on personal loyalties maintained by sharing out the spoils of war. It was the core of the feudal political system and is the paradigm of the relationships that underpin today's global corporatism. The corporate "committee" is today's *comitatus*, and it is the basis for a lack of responsibility in a corporate system of "limited liability".

Chapter 6 details the implications of the "military entertainment complex". There is an unbroken history of cooperation in the United States among the institutions of war and those of entertainment beginning with the CPI. The upshot of that institutional marriage in the United States is the global and universally pervasive extent of contemporary militarisation. Today we cannot neatly separate military organisation along public–private lines, between individual and collective interests, or between general cultural activity and specifically military activity. The influence of entertainmentised militarisation of our current institutions cannot be isolated as something apart from mundane settings. As if to underscore the significance of that history, the newly elected president of the United States is a reality television star who drives the news cycle with abusive tweets from his personal cell phone, attacking individuals and nation-states without distinction.

Chapter 7 draws together the themes of the book to argue the importance of understanding the arc I describe here. The means, methods, and logic of the CPI are central to the development of what I describe as neofeudal corporatism, just as they were to the development of the United States as a world military power. What becomes evident, as Kenneth Burke points out, is that war is an ultimate and special case of human cooperation, a tragic and sacrificial potlatch of social unity and shared purpose. That is to say: war requires cooperation, communication, and coordination in the highest degrees of intensity. One might therefore go further, as Burke does, to suggest that war depends on a perverse kind of love. After a century of being subjected to constant, rhetorically propagated crises, political systems everywhere are showing signs of breaking down. Political and economic scenes are depleted and depressing, worn to the nub with the endless anxieties borne of eternal crisis. The "hot button" and "wedge" issues that divide and anger people are played by political and media interests in pursuit of money or power, or both. People are admonished to "be their own brand", to "broadcast themselves", to be a part of television's "reality", a social media "star". The kind of selfish and egoistic ethos that those imperatives encourage are evident in the behaviour of the new American president. Individuals are hunted and bombed as if they were warring nation-states. Ambition, competition, aggression, hubris, and outrage are schooled in formal and informal ways, within and beyond the institutions of the crumbling state.

Nothing exemplifies the status of blatant hubris and outright hostility more than current political affairs. Throughout allegedly developed democracies, political systems have steadily deteriorated into cynical vacuums, tightly tuned to the most flagrantly corrupt practices to the point at which a reality television star advocating totalitarian policies can become president of the world's most powerful nation. Environmental catastrophe looms ever larger, while corporate benefices continue apace, pouring billions into lobbying efforts aimed at ensuring nothing is done to stem rising social and economic inequality, the decline of political and personal responsibility, or the expansion of militarism throughout every pore of the bodies politic involved. It is egosystem versus ecosystem. Questions of truth have never been so insignificant in comparison with the problems of action and ethics. From Trump, to Brexit, to the International Monetary Fund's moral and monetary failures in Greece, indications are that current political economic arrangements are at the point of total collapse. Throughout the Creel century, the fix for such states of decay has been to instigate total war in protection of the status quo. Instigation is always a matter of rhetoric. And so this book ends with a plea for rhetoric, for a rhetorical understanding of language, for an approach to strategized communication that first asks, not whether the communique is true, but what it is trying to do by way of action, at whom the action is aimed, and to which ends it is aimed.

Note

1 Graham and Luke (2003, 2005, 2011); Graham and Hearn (2010); Graham (2006); Graham (2002, 2001); Graham, Keenan, and Dowd (2004).

2 National Disunity in an Age of New Human Sciences

The culture into which the Creel Committee was introduced was turbulent and divided. From 1865 to 1900, 100 million immigrants had entered the United States. From 1900 onwards, immigration was running steady at a million per year, with most coming from throughout Europe. Business had already gotten "big", with the rapid rise and fall of Standard Oil, which began a series of federal "trust-busting" legislative reforms that would continue into the 1920s. Government was an intensely local affair, with the federal government having relatively few powers compared to those it exercises today. Corruption and nepotism were rife at local and state levels, ethnic divisions were at an all-time high, and mechanised industrialism was laying waste to older patterns of life. The intellectual environment was also in revolution. Science was delivering the goods. New material achievements abounded at an unprecedented rate. The holy trinity of the day was science, money, and efficiency. Those elements constituted the "rhetorical field" of the era, the hierarchy of cultural institutions with which people identified or against which they reacted. The impersonal, objective, and efficient values as measured by money and science were widely seen as the path to social progress. Standing in its way were the evils of division, corruption, and waste.

When we look into the period leading up to the CPI's establishment, we find ourselves at the heart of Progressive Era US politics (1898–1920). The "things" of science had been flourishing in abundance in America since the mid-19th century. The telegraph, phonograph, the Panama Canal, the assembly line, the aeroplane, and the telephone were just a few of the marvels that were emblematic of an age of rapid technical development. The world was fast becoming electrified, motorised, wireless, and airborne. Yet despite science delivering so well in the material world of machinery, the human world of the day was dominated by perceptions of inefficiency, corruption, exploitation, and waste (Callahan, 1962, Ch. 1). The United States were far from united in any systematic or practical sense. Ballard

Campbell (2014) notes the intense localism evident in 1890, with 30,000 'general-purpose local governments' and '100,000 special-purpose bodies, primarily school districts' raising taxes in towns, townships, and villages throughout the country (p. 17). The federal government exercised relatively few powers. They largely consisted of

> the conduct of diplomatic relations, the maintenance of a military, the distribution of the public lands, the operation of a rudimentary postal system, the collection of certain taxes, the regulation of a handful of commercial activities, and the support of a small administrative establishment.
>
> (pp. 18–19)

The bulk of legislation was instead carried out within state and local jurisdictions, with the state legislating on issues from interest rates to voting rights to policies affecting issues of gender and race (p. 19). Geographically, though, the national government had built 'a territorial state that stretched from the Atlantic to the Pacific coasts' (p. 19).

The character of the US federal government at the turn of the 20th century is barely recognisable to the contemporary eye. Grover Cleveland (1885–1889, 1893–1897) answered the White House phone and 'sometimes the doorbell' (Campbell, 2014, p. 24). The states had no large bureaucracies, placing those functions in the hands of independent commissions and boards. Illinois alone had 100 such entities operating by 1914 (p. 25). Positions on them were often granted on the basis of patronage and nepotism. The graft and corruption associated with such arrangements were widespread, becoming the subject of reform movements beginning in the 1840s and reaching a crescendo from 1902 through to the 1910s (Callahan, 1962). Campbell (2014) details the kinds of corruption the extreme localism of the era fostered. He describes law enforcement arrangements in Birmingham, Alabama, around 1891, which had sheriffs on commission in a system of shanghai and human traffic:

> Instead of receiving a salary, sheriffs derived their income from fees for making arrests and fines levied on the guilty. People unable to pay were sentenced to hard labor; convictions for gambling drew a hundred days. The sheriff could lease convicts to coal and iron companies in the county, a practice that the Birmingham police also followed. To keep up with industrialists' steady demand for cheap labor, the sheriff hired deputies by private arrangement. The chief duty of these assistants was to conduct dragnets among the idle class, as the black community was stereotyped.
>
> (Campbell, 2014, p. 13)

Broad-ranging and entrenched levels of corruption, a burgeoning suffragette movement, disruptive levels of immigration, a fast proliferating class
of robber barons, the rapid rise of big business, and a growing public appe-
tite for "social justice" and "reform" provided fertile ground for the emergence of a journalism that was to be labelled by Theodor Roosevelt in 1906
as 'muckraking', an approach known today as 'investigative journalism'
(Neuzil, 1996).

The Muckrake

Essentially a 'progressive reform' movement, muckraking journalism concerned itself with 'municipal corruption', 'violence against nonstriking coal
miners by striking unionists', the underhand tactics of big business, and
asserted the general idea that American citizens were victims of 'collective
thievery', 'a conspiracy of greed perpetuated by businesses, public officials,
and unionists' (Landers, 2013, p. 222). According to Arthur and Leila Weinberg
(1961/2001)

> The muckrake touched practically every phase of American life; noth-
> ing was immune from it. The flaws were photographed, analyzed,
> pinpointed. The men [*sic*] engaged in muckraking were bold. Their
> accusations were specific, direct. Names were named They pointed
> to sore spots in business, in politics. They found food adulteration,
> unscrupulous practices in finance and insurance companies, fraudulent
> claims for and injurious ingredients in patent medicines, rape of natural
> resources, bureaucracy, prostitution, a link between government and
> vice. Prison conditions were exposed, as were newspapers and their
> domination by advertisers. The church was not spared from the muck-
> rakers' probing, particularly the famous, highly revered Trinity Church
> of New York and its tenement houses. The evils of child labor were
> exposed.
>
> (p. xxiii)

The muckraker movement had political teeth. Ida Tarbell (1857–1944), who
was according to many the first investigative journalist, is credited with
single-handedly triggering the investigation and subsequent break up of J.
D. Rockefeller's Standard Oil Trust (Tarbell, 1902). In 1890, it was 'the
most powerful business on earth, controlling 90 percent of the nation's oil
market and nearly 80 percent of the world's' (Reitman, 1998).

Tarbell was as much a product of the scientific age as the array of new
methods, machines, and ideas shaping the United States at the time. Her journalism combined scientific method with excellent schooling in the trivium

of rhetoric, grammar, and logic (Brady, 1984, p. 21). Her approach to journalism was a form of 'research' through which '["capital T"] Truth about the actions and motivations of powerful people could be discovered' and was based on the idea that such truths 'could be conveyed in such a way as to precipitate meaningful social change' (Weinberg, 2008, p. 15). The 'scientific' method and effects of Tarbell's (1902) *History of The Standard Oil Company*, resulting as it did in the company's demise, redefined journalism, giving a new, national scope to its social, cultural, and political functions. It is worth noting the place of science in the method of the muckrakers for two reasons. First is that Creel was counted among the muckraker's ranks during his time as owner and editor of *The Independent* newspaper in Kansas. Second, Creel (1920) would maintain to the end of his days that the entire CPI enterprise was scientific, at least so far as it was concerned solely with the dissemination of unbiased facts.

Also noteworthy are the technical means that underpinned the national influence of the muckrakers. Feldstein (2006) notes with irony that the movement's national scope and influence was 'made possible by the very industrialized capitalism that the muckrakers exposed', especially 'the transcontinental railroad' that allowed 'national distribution and marketing, which in turn created a demand for nationwide advertising and thus the first mass-circulation national news publications' (p. 5). The ironic implications of the movement's power were not lost on Randolph Hearst either, at that point a Congressman and owner of several powerful, though locally limited, publications. He saw the political power of the new journalistic approach and used it in an ongoing battle against Theodore Roosevelt to challenge for the US Presidency.

It was during that battle, and in response to it, that Roosevelt in 1906 gave the new journalistic movement the pejorative label of muckraker (Neuzil, 1996). Roosevelt first became president following the assassination of William McKinley in 1901. He blamed inflammatory rhetoric in the news media for McKinley's death, with Hearst's *New York Journal* publishing a poem by Ambrose Bierce 'that seemed to promote McKinley's assassination' (p. 30). Hearst bought his first nationally influential title, *Cosmopolitan*, in 1905, which featured serialised muckraking pieces such as 'The Treason of the Senate' and other pieces identifying Roosevelt's Republican Party as 'the tool of the trusts' (pp. 30–31). Hearst demonstrates an awareness of a scientism growing in importance. Commenting on the 'Treason of the Senate' series to its author, David Phillips, he said 'I had intended an exposé. We have merely an attack. . . . The facts, the proof, the documentary evidence are an important thing, and the article is deficient in them. We want more definite facts throughout' (p. 32). Facts were the order of the day. As long as the facts were in evidence, it was assumed that science would deliver dividends.

Scientific Government

The new enthusiasm for the benefits of science went well beyond the purely mechanical. Science would bring order, understanding, and predictable modification to the human world. Woodrow Wilson contributed greatly to the movement by proposing in 1887 the 'scientific administration' of government aimed at discovering 'what government can do' and how to do those things 'at the least possible cost of money or of energy' (1887, p. 197). He notes the complexities of governing compared to earlier times that need to be addressed: corruption at local levels of government, a highly decentralised country, the rising power of large monopolies in business, and the lack of 'impartial scientific method' in American administration (p. 201). He frames the main issues as ones of culture, pointing out that all available approaches to administration employ 'only foreign tongues' and 'utters none but what are to our minds alien ideas' (p. 202). He slates that alien character to the history of absolutism in Europe as compared with the democratic foundations of America, noting that even with democratic constitutions following the revolutionary period, the administrative structures of continental Europe continued their despotism 'by becoming paternal. They made themselves too efficient to be dispensed with, too smoothly operative to be noticed, too enlightened to be inconsiderately questioned, too benevolent to be suspected, too powerful to be coped with' (p. 203).

Wilson displays a keen awareness of rhetoric. In the conduct of scientific administration, it becomes necessary to 'instruct and persuade a multitudinous monarch called public opinion—a much less feasible undertaking than to influence a single monarch called a king' (p. 207). Democracy therefore becomes in large part a problem of rhetoric, of managing public opinion:

> Whoever would effect a change in a modern constitutional government must first educate his fellow-citizens to want some change. That done, he must persuade them to want the particular change he wants. He must first make public opinion willing to listen and then see to it that it listen to the right things. He must stir it up to search for an opinion, and then manage to put the right opinion in its way.
>
> (p. 208)

Wilson is so thoroughly concerned with public opinion as the central subject of democratic government he personifies the principle: 'In trying to instruct our own public opinion, we are dealing with a pupil apt to think itself quite sufficiently instructed beforehand' (p. 215). He is therefore concerned with increasing its 'efficiency' and reducing its potentially 'meddlesome' influences (p. 215). His answer is education, and he looks forward to the time 'when no college of respectability can afford to do without a well-filled chair of political science' (p. 215). Public opinion is the central plank of his scientific administration and the principle on which he would most insist: 'That principle is, that administration in the United States must be at all points sensitive to public opinion' (p. 216).

Wilson articulates what pragmatism means for administration: 'We do not study the art of governing: we govern' (p. 217). He assumes that efficient techniques of administration are transferable without consequence because of his distinction between politics as general principles and administration as application of those principles in specific contexts:

> When we study the administrative systems of France and Germany, knowing that we are not in search of political principles, we need not care a peppercorn for the constitutional or political reasons which Frenchmen or Germans give for their practices when explaining them to us. If I see a murderous fellow sharpening a knife cleverly, I can borrow his way of sharpening the knife without borrowing his probable intention to commit murder with it; and so, if I see a monarchist dyed in the wool managing a public bureau well, I can learn his business methods without changing one of my republican spots. . . . We can thus scrutinize the anatomy of foreign governments without fear of getting any of their diseases into our veins; dissect alien systems without apprehension of blood-poisoning.
>
> (1887, p. 220)

Here we come upon the isolation of technique from principle so common to pragmatisms of every stripe. Wilson assumes that administration is a wholly technical problem. But like rhetoric, administration is a 'logological' pursuit; its operations are conducted solely within the realm of words (Burke, 1961). Yet even more thoroughly than rhetoric, the words of administration aim to have real effects on people, processes, and relationships beyond the world of words.

It is here that I think an important distinction becomes apparent. Up to the present day, the perception has long been common that techniques, technologies, and tools are interchangeable terms, or even the same thing. That is not the case in relation to verbal techniques, which are simultaneously Agencies (means) and Acts (action) (Burke, 1945/1961). In the case of rhetoric and administration, Purpose (intention) must also be present. Wilson's mistake here is to assume that a tool (a thing to be used as part of technique) necessarily has a definite purpose outside technique (how it is to be used) and technology (literally, the logic of technique; the *reason* for using it): tool, technique, technology. They are as different as means, method, and methodology. There is a more serious implication in the terminological conflation of tool, technique, and technology. By using "technology" to describe tools, techniques, *and* technologies, the motives for using a given tool or technique are automatically obscured, which means that the elements of choice and ethics are also obscured.

In 'logological' cases, tool, technique, and technology are all of a piece (Burke, 1961). You cannot have one without the other. Rhetoric is again an excellent teacher on the point: the term '*artes sermonicales*—the speech arts' (Ong, 1971, p. 5) is identical in meaning to Aristotle's '*technē rhētorikē*', translated as *The Art of Rhetoric* (Aristotle, 1991). Rhetoric has multiple functions. That is given. But unless means, act, and purpose are united, there is no rhetoric. I think that this is the core of the scientistic age's great mistake: to understand language as a tool, separate from technique and technology, separate from what we do, an external "thing" to be used impartially, and confined to the realm of intellect, concept, and principle, despite pragmatism's orientation to the world of action. Contemporary usage of the term "technology" has been removed from its artistic, skilful origins to mean a class of "things" with which we do work: tools. The terminological conflation of tool, technique, and technology define the technocratic fallacy. So, taking up German or French techniques of administration meant also taking up their logic, tools, and ethics, whether Wilson wanted to or not. It is in fact a case of "politics be damned" for the sake of "efficient" administration. That is not to say we cannot separate tool, technique, and technology in many cases, as in golf club (tool), swing (technique), and study of the swing (technology), or in Wilson's metaphor, the knife, its sharpening, and the study of the sharpening technique. But in the purposive, active, rhetorical realm of language as social action, there is no "efficient" means to separate them without doing moral violence to speaker, speech, and socius.

The Efficient Management of Bodies, Minds, and Movements

It was through the lens of pragmatism that scientific journalism, advertising, administration, management, psychology, and education came into focus as both desirable and necessary in the United States at the turn of the 20th century. The need for efficiency was made more urgent by the rapidly urbanising, massifying, and diversifying social and cultural landscapes of the country, along with the national scale reporting of systemic failures by the muckraker movement. Perhaps nobody before or since has had the far-reaching effect on the industrial rhetorical environment as Frederick Winslow Taylor. In 1911, he spelled out the aim of scientific management to a national audience:

In the past the man has been first; in the future the system must be first. This in no sense, however, implies that great men are not needed. On the contrary, the first object of any good system must be that of developing first-class men; and under systematic management the best man rises to the top more certainly and more rapidly than ever before.

(Taylor, 1911, p. 7)

Taylor's first public formulation of 'the system' was in 1895, eight years after Wilson's argument for scientific administration. His system was developed on the 'shop floor' of American steel mills. Again, in apparent irony, the aim of his system, which would unleash historically unprecedented industrial growth and eventually bring the world to the brink of total environmental collapse, was to conserve natural resources (Taylor, 1911, p. 5). That included people's energies, but those, Taylor noticed, were harder to see being wasted (pp. 5–6). His solution was time and motion studies to design the 'one best way' to do any given job (Taylor, 1911). Taylor argued up 'the system' as being applicable well beyond the realm of the factory floor. In his view, 'the best management is a true science, resting upon clearly defined laws, rules, and principles, as a foundation' and its principles 'are applicable to all kinds of human activities, from our simplest individual acts to the work of our great corporations' (p. 7). The principles 'should apply with equal force to all social activities' including 'homes', 'farms', 'the business of our tradesmen', 'churches', 'philanthropic institutions', 'universities', and 'governmental departments' (p. 8). His system thus has the endemic characteristic of pragmatic scientism that separates theory from practice. It 'consists of certain broad general principles . . . which can be applied in many ways' and any description of the best techniques 'should in no way be confused with the principles themselves' (pp. 28–29).

Taylor's is a moral endeavour. He aims to lessen the effects of some people being 'born lazy or inefficient' and others being 'born greedy and brutal' (Taylor, 1911, p. 30). While he sees 'vice and crime' as endemic to the human condition, he claims that people will be 'far more prosperous, far happier, and more free from discord and dissension' working within his system. His advocacy proceeds from an interesting direction, namely a critique of the 'mass of traditional knowledge', hitherto uncodified, held by any given class of workers about any given task or job (p. 32). That kind of codifying impulse is evident throughout the history of technical developments from the translation of Homer into written form in ancient Greece (Havelock, 1986), the systematic stitching together of dispersed cottage industry by proto-capitalists across Western Europe (Weber, 1930/1992), the gathering of folk tales by the Brothers Grimm (Zipes, 2014), and the numerous translations of folk songs into classical music by the likes of Greig,

Stravinsky, and Bartôk (cf. Gilbert, 1917; Suchoff, 1972). Taylor describes his work as pooling a mass of historical and oral knowledge about work and codifying it within a systematic framework, indicating that his management system is as much a cultural endeavour as a technical one.

An industrial eugenics informs Taylor. His research was consistently aimed at finding the 'first-class man' and codifying how he worked. Just as there were born first-class management types, he thought, there were also born first-class pig iron handlers, like the now-famous 'Schmidt', whom Taylor described as being born 'so stupid that he was unfitted to do most kinds of laboring work' (Taylor, 1911, p. 62; cf. also Callahan, 1962, Ch. 2). Anyone born to carry pig iron would necessarily be 'so stupid that the word "percentage" has no meaning to him' and so he would need training by someone more intelligent 'into the habit of working in accordance with the laws of this science before he can be successful' (p. 59). There are natural born managers and natural born 'ox' type of people (p. 62). Yet even with such a view of his workers, Taylor was convinced that under scientific management, workers 'looked upon the men who were over them, their bosses and their teachers, as their very best friends' (p. 72). He takes the scientific mindset into dramatistic regions with the idea that the next stage of scientific management requires 'the accurate study of the motives which influence men' (p. 119; cf. Burke, 1945/1962).

The mind was also considered susceptible to scientific control. The behaviourism of John B. Watson made an instant impact upon psychology with an approach aimed explicitly at predicting and controlling behaviour and erasing the line between humans and other animals.

> Psychology as the behaviorist views it is a purely objective experi-mental branch of natural science. Its theoretical goal is the predic-tion and control of behavior. Introspection forms no essential part of its methods, nor is the scientific value of its data dependent upon the readiness with which they lend themselves to interpretation in terms of consciousness. The behaviorist, in his efforts to get a unitary scheme of animal response, recognizes no dividing line between man and brute.
> (Watson, 1913/1994, p. 248)

Watson's behaviourist psychology fit well with the Progressive Era's 'visions of social control', 'a belief that the ills of the world rested on the environment, and a belief that with the assistance of "science," man could construct and reconstruct his world' (Kesher, 1990, p. 50). Watson would go on to become a major force in J. Walter Thompson during the 1920s, the world's largest advertising agency at the time.

Advertising was also getting the scientific treatment in the early years of the 20th century. The following comes from Herbert Casson (1911) who enthusiastically applies Taylor's system to advertising and sales. He notes that the principles of efficiency had first been applied by Moltke with great success in the Franco–Prussian war of 1870, that its application to machinery and production by the likes of Taylor had also shown outstanding dividends and that its application by the US military had also been met with unquestionable success. With scientific management, Casson sees that efficiency is now 'doing with WORKERS what inventors have already done with machinery' (p. 4). It is entirely a matter of scientific method, it 'is not a mere guess or fancy, as most of our "truth" is. It has a solid foundation of facts' (Casson, 1911, p. 5). Noting once again the recurring emphasis on 'facts' in all such theorisations of the era, it is worth at this point considering Veblen's (1906) perspective on the fast-emerging scientism that had insinuated itself into almost every domain of organised human action, including education, psychology, management, public administration, journalism, advertising, and public relations.

Science, Pragmatism, and the Triumph of Method

Veblen (1906) describes the implications of what he saw as a 'matter-of-fact' culture emerging in 'modern civilization' under the sign of science. He makes a clear distinction between the provenances of science and the provenances of pragmatic knowledge. Science is a descendent of idle curiosity, 'most closely related to the aptitude for play', a form of speculative thought that is and was always 'without teleology', yet which is always dramatised according to canons of power and success, the organising patterns of material advantage, evident at any given point in history. Among the provenances of science, he counts various types of 'myth-making, folklore, and occult symbolising'; 'creative arts'; and 'metaphysical insight and dialectical versatility' (p. 589). Idle curiosity responds to stimuli not pragmatically, which is to say not 'in terms of an expedient line of conduct', but rather 'in terms of the sequence of activities going on in the observed phenomena' (p. 590). He argues that this aspect of what came to be known as science, a singular focus on causes and effects, is always 'dramatised' in terms of the dominant cultural institutions of the day. The means of scientific dramatisation is an excellent indicator of what might be termed the "cultural episteme", but which I name here the "rhetorical field".

Veblen (1906) gives an historical account of the modes of dramatisation that have characterised the products of idle curiosity throughout history. The most ancient approach is to dramatize science in terms of 'life histories', 'the broad vital principle of generation', concerned with '[p]rocreation, birth, growth, and decay' (p. 592). The form of dramatisation focuses on 'the cycle of postulates within which the dramatised processes of natural phenomena run their course. Creation is procreation in these archaic theoretical systems, and causation is gestation and birth' (p. 592). So long as the ruling institutions are ones of 'blood-relationship, descent, and clannish discriminations', so too are 'the canons of knowledge' dramatised in related ways. Later, when the institutions become more baroque and arbitrary, dominated by the whims of kings and other tyrants in systems 'involving mastery and servitude, gradations of privilege and honor, coercion and personal dependence, then the scheme of knowledge undergoes an analogous change' (p. 593). We see well recorded relationships between successive cultural hierarchies and the changing dramatisation of cause and effect (science). For the mediaeval system, the canons guiding idle curiosity are 'graded dignity, authenticity, and dependence', the cosmologies of the age are cast 'in terms of a feudalistic hierarchy of agents and elements', and the laws of nature 'are sought in terms of authoritative enactment', such as those proper to gods and kings. Similarly, success in the early modern scientific era 'is a matter of workmanship' as it has been in no other era, and the deity moves from being cast as a 'suzerain concerned with his own prestige' to become a workman like creator engaged in making useful things 'for man', a 'talented mechanic' (p. 596). Consequently, 'the "natural laws"' detailed by scientists of the age 'are no longer decrees of a preternatural legislative authority, but rather details of the workshop specifications handed down by the master-craftsman for the guidance of handicraftsmen working out his designs' (p. 596).

In the machine age, Veblen (1906) argues, the causes at work are conceived of in 'a highly impersonal way' (p. 596). Yet dramatisation of events continues, even in such a highly impersonal formulation. Activity is 'not a fact of observation, but is imputed to the phenomena by the observer' (p. 596). The machine dominates political and economic scenes. Its industrial implementation had delivered unprecedented levels of private wealth and power and become 'a cultural force of wide-reaching consequence', and so 'the formulations of science have made another move in the direction of impersonal matter-of-fact'. This is the point at which pragmatic and scientific knowledge get confounded because, for the first time in history, scientific knowledge becomes, at a visible level, indistinguishable from pragmatic knowledge. But that is sheer accident:

> The reason why scientific theories can be turned to account for these practical ends is not that these ends are included in the scope of scientific inquiry. These useful purposes lie outside the scientist's interest. It is not that he aims, or can aim, at technological improvements. His inquiry is as "idle" as that of the Pueblo myth-maker. But the canons

of validity under whose guidance he works are those imposed by the modern technology, through habituation to its requirements; and therefore his results are available for the technological purpose. His canons of validity are made for him by the cultural situation; they are habits of thought imposed on him by the scheme of life current in the community in which he lives; and under modern conditions this scheme of life is largely machine-made. In the modern culture, industry, industrial processes, and industrial products have progressively gained upon humanity, until these creations of man's ingenuity have latterly come to take the dominant place in the cultural scheme; and it is not too much to say that they have become the chief force in shaping men's daily life, and therefore the chief factor in shaping men's habits of thought. Hence men have learned to think in the terms in which the technological processes act.

(p. 598)

Veblen (1906) demonstrates that the provenance of pragmatic knowledge is entirely different from that of science. Pragmatic knowledge is and has always been a matter of survival, of learning how to live in the world, what Veblen calls 'worldly wisdom'. It is therefore purposive (teleological) and by definition directed at use. Veblen defines pragmatic knowledge as being 'designed to serve an expedient end for the knower' (p. 591). He makes the distinction to serve the 'need of a simple term by which to mark the distinction between worldly wisdom and idle learning' (p. 591). Because it is directed at specific ends, pragmatic knowledge is by definition not science, no matter how systematic or methodical it might be. It is simply a means to a predetermined end. If the end of any method is a known expedient before the inquiry begins, it is pragmatically oriented. If it is an inquiry that proceeds from idle curiosity, then it is scientifically oriented.

Hence the startling conclusion that Veblen draws: even as scientific and pragmatic knowledge seem to merge in the machine paradigm, in as much as they seem concerned with the same domains, they are in fact further apart than they have been in all human history. Science can inform pragmatic knowledge and its machine-based industry, but the reverse is not the case. Technology 'makes use of the same range of concepts, thinks in the same terms, and applies the same tests of validity as modern science. In both, the terms of standardization, validity, and finality are always terms of impersonal sequence' (Veblen, 1906, p. 598). In short, the chasm between the two is this: 'Pragmatism creates nothing but maxims of expedient conduct. Science creates nothing but theories' (p. 600). Science 'knows nothing of policy or utility, of better or worse', whereas pragmatic knowledge 'does not contribute to the advance of a knowledge of fact' and only an 'incidental bearing on scientific research' mainly as 'inhibition and misdirection'. In fact, Veblen argues, where 'canons of expediency' are allowed to interfere with scientific inquiry, 'the consequence is an unhappy one for science, however happy it may be for some other purpose extraneous to science'. Pragmatic wisdom 'is at cross-purposes with the disinterested scientific spirit, and the pursuit of it induces an intellectual bias that is incompatible with scientific insight' (p. 600). Thus, argues Veblen, the pragmatic mindset, once culturally dominant, colours culture similarly to the 'barbaric past'. That is, the culture becomes hostile to anything other than pragmatic expedients and inhibits to the point of elimination 'all effective aptitude for other than worldly wisdom' (p. 603). In such situations, the culture 'has selectively worked out a temperamental bias and a scheme of life from which objective, matter-of-fact knowledge is virtually excluded in favor of pragmatism, secular and religious' (p. 603).

Pragmatism, Scientism, and the Progressive Era

The various confusions among science, method, technology, and knowledge in evidence in early 20th century America can be explained by the rise of pragmatism as the philosophical foundations of American scientism. William James' influence is perhaps most widely in evidence. He says that pragmatism 'does not stand for any special results. It is a method only' (1907, p. 20). He sees it bringing science and metaphysics to the point at which they 'would in fact work absolutely hand in hand' (p. 20). The pragmatic theory of truth is related to the influx of 'new facts'. Their influx is a fact in itself. However, those facts are not truth as such: 'Truth *is what we say about* them' (p. 25)[1]. Thus, the two parts of pragmatism are, 'first, a method; and second, a genetic theory of what is meant by truth' (p. 26). Pragmatists 'talk about truths in the plural, about their utility and satisfactoriness, about the success with which they "work", etc.' (p. 27). James goes so far as to say that pragmatism, 'devoted though she may be to facts', has no materialist bias and can therefore accommodate theological ideas to the degree that they prove practical and useful: '*If theological ideas prove to have a value for concrete life, they will be true, for pragmatism, in the sense of being good for so much. For how much more they are true, will depend entirely on their relations to other truths that also have to be acknowledged*' (p. 29, italics in original). To put the point clearly, James says that, according to pragmatics, 'an idea is "true" so long as to believe it profitable to our lives. That it is *good*, for as much as it profits' (p. 30). The true '*is the name of whatever proves itself to be good in the way of belief, and good, too, for definite, assignable reasons*' (p. 30). And therefore, it becomes the case that 'what is better for us to believe is true *unless the belief incidentally clashes with some other vital benefit*' (p. 31). For pragmatics, the 'only test of probable truth is what works best in the way of leading us, what fits every part of life best and combines with the collectivity of experience's demands, nothing being omitted' (p. 32).

As I show in the following chapter, the pragmatic conception of fact is actually rhetoric in scientific guise. I should be clear that although I select James as being of special interest here based largely on his influence, pragmatics was not at the time, nor is it now, a unified field of thought. Ralph Barton Perry argues that the 'modern movement known as pragmatism is largely the result of James' misunderstanding of Peirce' (in Burke, 1937/1984, p. 9). James' "cash value" of an idea has itself been the subject of reams of argument. It is an undoubtedly metaphorical statement. The point I wish to make here is that, as a way of understanding the world at the turn of the 20th century, James' pragmatism exemplifies Veblen on the historical relationships between worldly knowledge, science, and the cultural hierarchies of the day. In James' formulation, there is no distinction between generals and particulars, no thought that is not oriented towards a specific end, and no knowledge that counts other than as it profits the person who believes it. Abstraction is outlawed, or rather denied. Method and philosophy are confounded, as are method and science. The end of James' pragmatics is profit, however conceived. Its sole standard is "what works" for any given purpose. Truth is not a category; it is what we say it is, based on whether it is good for us to believe it or not. James' use of "cash value", "profit", a fact-based means of controlling the external world, and what boils down to an "efficiency" view of truth almost perfectly mirrors the workings of machine industry; the ethos of the mega-businesses that are at that point the extensions of individuals like Hearst, Rockefeller, Morgan, and others; and a view of science that sees itself as being at all times either totally applied or utterly worthless.

The dedication to facts in every field of organisation, including the mass organisation of communication, is in evidence everywhere throughout Progressive Era discourse leading up to the establishment of the CPI, which would also run along the lines of scientific management (Brewer, 2009, p. 85). So too with scientific prediction and control of people. Just as today, with the emphasis and reliance on "big data" starting to grip the broader imagination, the Creel century started in a world dominated by the idea that scientifically generated facts could solve every problem, that human beings could be organised and controlled scientifically, that facts must form the basis of that control, and that efficiency was the guiding standard of all work.

Note

1 Throughout the manuscript, italics in any quoted material are in the original unless otherwise noted.

3   Theorising the CPI

There is a strong tendency to think that the Committee on Public Information (CPI) created something entirely new. Certainly nothing like it had ever happened before. But the novelties the CPI introduced were qualitative and structural, not formal or perhaps even quantitative other than organisationally. As we saw in the previous chapter, a national self-consciousness had started to emerge in the United States, especially with progressive politics and the muckrake and the way in which the idea of "reform" drew together multiple, diverse, and conflicting populations at a national level around problems that were national in scale and character. That is not to say those populations agreed on anything, but just that they had come to collectively focus on problems identified by the muckrakers, and that from whichever side of whichever problem, the general consensus was that things had to change. The private sector had begun to operate with influence on a national scale in areas that were largely foreign to the federal government, or at least very new in the cases where federal powers had started to expand during the 17 years between the turn-of-the-century muckrake and the time at which the CPI was established. Public opinion had begun to assert itself as a political force and the rhetorically sensitive Wilson had named "it" as the erstwhile monarch of democracy and therefore as something that implicitly needed managing. With the widespread emphasis on scientism and its facts, and the relegation of rhetoric to history, Creel was free to weaponise rhetoric.

The aim of this chapter is to theorise the CPI's activities and present an explanatory lens that makes its long-lasting and profound effects comprehensible. Because the activities of the CPI were aimed at persuasion, the lens requires a rhetorical dimension. Because CPI was aimed at the national level, it requires a dimension that can cope with the notion of a mass consciousness indicated by the term "national public opinion". Because it was aimed at bringing the country to war, the theory must allow for the extremes of life and death, of killing and being killed en masse. The rhetorical dimension is drawn from the approaches of Kenneth Burke (1950, 1961) and Walter Ong

(1971, 1977). The dimension theorising mass consciousness is drawn from Cooley (1909) and Bourdieu (1998). The theoretical dimension concerned with killing and being killed ties into the kinds of weaponised rhetoric Burke (1950) critiques in his *Rhetoric of Motives*. Needless to say, there are numerous technical, social, and cultural aspects to what the CPI did, but in the end, the three dimensions I name above were both necessary and sufficient to bring the country to war in ways that purely technical, social, and cultural aspects of the task were not. That is demonstrably the case when we look at later episodes that use the same approaches to rhetoric, mass consciousness, and mass murder to achieve both similar and more drastic results in entirely different technical, social, and cultural circumstances.

Rhetorics of Identifying, Bending, and Moving

Creel's project had to bring together a population profoundly divided along ethnic, class, religious, and geographic lines; transform the collective opinions and attitudes of that population such that they would approve of entering WWI on the side of the British Empire; and persuade an overwhelming majority of the population that it was right and good to send people to Europe to fight and die, for men to volunteer to do so in some cases, and for people to voluntarily engage in lesser sacrifices, such as buying bonds, working in munitions factories, or otherwise giving their lives and labour to the war effort. Those three rhetorical functions can be classified as identification, bending or turning people's attitudes, and moving people to action. The last two functions are typically treated together in Ciceronian strains of rhetoric (Ong, 1971). However, while attitude is necessary to action and is, as Burke describes it, incipient action, the taking on of an attitude is not sufficient in itself to be described as an act. That is to say, an attitude does not in itself qualify as action despite being a necessary *part* of action. In the case of the CPI, given its historical and cultural contexts described in the previous chapter, the special efforts that went into rhetorics of *flectere* (bending) and *movere* (moving) as consciously separate rhetorical effects require that they be treated separately here.

Identification: Dramatism and Logology

Scientistic analyses of meaning are testable only by standards of truth. Dramatistic analyses of meaning are concerned with what, how, why, and to what ends people are asked, encouraged, or coerced into doing specific things. A major test of persuasion is the differences between what people are expected to do and what they actually do in response to rhetorical efforts. As we saw in the previous chapter, the era into which the CPI was introduced was intensely scientistic. It was, as Veblen (1906) called it, a 'matter-of-fact' culture in which every problem was being addressed in terms of its value as worldly knowledge, which at that time had been confounded with science. In keeping with that aspect of the age, Creel (1920) is singular in his claims for the CPI as an institution that operated along totally fact-based, scientific lines. The emphasis on fact points directly to a 'eulogistic' camouflage for the various forms rhetoric in the CPI's methods (Bentham, 1824, p. 214, see also Burke, 1950). Unlike rhetoric, which had in the United States taken on a 'dyslogistic cast' because of its relation with "mere" opinion, the CPI's use of fact was indexical of 'moral approbation' because of its relationship to science (Bentham, p. 215).

Creel claimed in essence that the CPI did not seek to persuade; it merely presented the facts. In places the argument is quite explicit, but is worded throughout Creel's account of the CPI in many ways for many different audiences. The following comes from a request to neutral foreign governments to allow the CPI's news service to set up inside their jurisdictions:

> It is not the idea of the United States to conduct propaganda in neutral countries in the sense of attacking the motives and methods of the enemy, or in the nature of argument designed to compel or to persuade certain courses of conduct. Our activities in every neutral country are open and aboveboard, confined always to a very frank exposition of America's war aims, the nation's ideals, and future hopes.
>
> (Creel, 1920, p. 243)

Many of the criticisms of the CPI, beginning with Lippmann's, were based on Creel's assertions that the CPI did nothing other than present facts. Here is a typical statement by Creel on the news division:

> What was needed, and what we installed, was official machinery for the preparation and release of all news bearing upon America's war effort—not opinion nor conjecture, but *facts*—a running record of each day's progress in order that the fathers and mothers of the United States might gain a certain sense of partnership.
>
> (Creel, 1920, p. 72)

Creel makes the assertion that the CPI was a matter-of-fact organisation over and over:

> On the part of the press there was the fear, and a very natural one, that the new order of things meant "press agenting" on a huge scale. This fear could not be argued away, but had to be met by actual demonstration of

its groundlessness. Our job, therefore, was to present the facts without the slightest trace of color or bias, either in the selection of news or the manner in which it was presented.

(Creel, 1920, p. 73)

Creel is conducting what Burke calls 'a rhetoric in spite of itself'. The complete scientism with which Creel purported to undertake the work of the CPI stands in a naturally hostile relationship to notions of rhetoric and opinion. Opinion is the very soul of bias and presupposes bias as *prima materia*. Bias is what rhetoric aims at and what it draws on to achieve its ends. Opinion is based on probabilities and shares etymology with the word "option", both coming from a Proto Indo European (PIE) root meaning "to choose". The idea of judgements based on "likelihood" and choice takes on new and potent implications in the hands of pragmatic scientism and its standards of truth relative to the James' "cash value" of a fact.

The story of pragmatic facts begins with C. S. Peirce and his notion of 'verisimilitude', the most basic standard of truth in his pragmatism. For Peirce, truth in language is contingent whereas 'there can be no falsehood in conceptions' because they are, according to his definition, practically true, which is all that matters:

> *True* is an adjective applicable solely to representations and things considered as representations. It implies the agreement of the representation with its object. . . . I call this *verisimilitude*, and the representation a *copy*. . . . Resemblance consists in a likeness, which is a sameness of predicates. Carried to the highest point, it would *destroy* itself by becoming identity. All real resemblance, therefore, has a limit. Beyond the limits of resemblance, verisimilitude ceases. [Therefore] Verisimilitude is partial truth.

(Peirce, 1861, p. 21)

Peirce steps through a hierarchy of truth in which verisimilitude is the 'simplest kind of agreement of truth', and since it is necessarily incomplete and refers only to representations, it is also paradoxically a valid description of false representations. Since conceptions cannot be false, he argues that the truth of conceptions cannot be verisimilitude (1861, p. 21). The next order of truth agreement is 'veracity', a 'constant connection between a sign and a thing', a convention, such that the thing cannot reliably appear without its sign. Moreover, he says, because signs and their concepts take time to become conventionalised, and because conceptions are true from the beginning, 'the truth of conceptions is not *veracity*' (p. 21). The truth of conceptions is of a different order. Peirce defines the near perfection of verisimilitude and veracity as being based on an invariable connection, and therefore a 'unity of substance' between the nature of things and their representations. He calls the perfection 'verity' and its representation a 'type' (p. 22). Since, he says, 'conceptions perfectly correspond with qualities and since they have a connection therewith in the nature of things, they are *types* of things' (p. 22).

When considered from the distinctly different perspectives of dramatism and scientism, Peirce's practical philosophy of truth and all of its various children propagated by the likes of James, Dewey, Schiller, and others presents us with a notable paradox. The paradox is most clear in the following passage written by Peirce in 1906, at the height of US scientism. Peirce is talking about himself in the third person:

> Endeavoring, as a man of that type naturally would, to formulate what he so approved, he framed the theory that a conception, that is, the rational purport of a word or other expression, lies exclusively in its conceivable bearing upon the conduct of life; so that, since obviously nothing that might not result from experiment can have any direct bearing upon conduct, if one can define accurately all the conceivable experimental phenomena which the affirmation or denial of a concept could imply, one will have therein a complete definition of the concept, and there is absolutely *nothing more in it.*
>
> (Peirce, 1905, pp. 162–163)

The 'rational purport' of a concept, that is to say its "scientific", "reasonable", "philosophic", or "truth" value, is identical here to its 'direct bearing on conduct', in other words, its dramatistic value—or more specifically, *its value as a motive for action.* So, for Peirce, the scientistic value of a concept is identical to its dramatistic value. Yet the different parts of reality those two speak of are entirely different in language and life. Peirce goes further and sets the propositional manifestation of a concept within the specifics of the tense system, placing it into realms well beyond the strictly scientistic:

> The rational meaning of every proposition lies in the future. . . . It is, according to the pragmaticist, that form in which the proposition becomes applicable to human conduct, not in these or those special circumstances, nor when one entertains this or that special design, but that form which is most directly applicable to self-control under every situation, and to every purpose. This is why he locates the meaning in future time; for future conduct is the only conduct that is subject to self-control. But in order that that form of the proposition which is to be taken as its meaning should be applicable to every situation and

to every purpose upon which the proposition has any bearing, it must be simply the general description of all the experimental phenomena which the assertion of the proposition virtually predicts.

(Pierce, 1905, pp. 173–174)

The futuristic orientation of Peirce's propositions, and especially that he designates to them the function of controlling conduct in the future tense (the only place in time conduct can be directed, controlled, or altered) and assigns to them a non-finite range of purposes, moves their functions into the realm of the normative proposal, and is therefore an ethical and rhetorical formulation of truth rather than a propositional one. The point of view extends through to James, Dewey, and beyond, and the paradox is carried throughout the various schools of American pragmatism. Dewey is quite plain that pragmatism is 'instrumental in furnishing points of view and working ideas which may clarify and illuminate the actual and concrete course of life' (Dewey, 1905, p. 77, as cited in Pratt, 2002, p. 11).

The implications are too numerous to go into here. But for our present purposes, we can say that James, Dewey, and Peirce are espousing a propositional form of language that functions in an entirely rhetorical way. That is, while the truths of pragmatism take the form of a proposition (a statement testable by standards of truth), what designates them as *being* truthful is a requirement for them to function as proposals for future action, that is, as implicit exhortations (Graham, 2006). Further, when we add to this James' (1907) emphasis on the methodical discovery of facts as the basis for any propositional formation in pragmatics, we encounter a collapse of theory into method and purpose, a simultaneous metaphorical transfer of proposition (statement of truth) into proposal (exhortation to action), and thereby into a covert rhetoric. Within the framing of an essentially rhetorical outcome as the scientific standard of pragmatism, the systematic functional metaphor established between proposition and proposal achieves a number of important ends in the context of the CPI's efforts and its later influences. First, the emphasis on "fact" provides total cover for the rhetorical ends associated with the CPI's truth statements. Second, being ostensibly fact based and entirely matter-of-fact in its presentation, the method of pragmatism presents as "science" or "scientific" that which is functionally rhetorical. Third, by subjecting all fact-getting to the singular test of effects in the world in respect of future human action, the propositions of pragmatism respond solely to tests that are in effect rhetorical and therefore probabilistic. Creel used the pragmatic paradox of rhetorical-scientific facts to go to work on the broken body politic of America.

Bodies politic can be militarised or pacified, they can be persuaded of purposes, attitudes, and acts of all kinds (Graham and Luke, 2003). Cooley (1909) and Bourdieu (1998) provide grounds for a perspective that can see non-individualistic levels of cognition at work. Cooley puts the issue succinctly: 'When we study the social mind we merely fix our attention on larger aspects and relations rather than on the narrower ones of ordinary psychology' (1909, p. 3). Social cognition can be theorised from the perspective of links between habits, habitus, social context, and social history (Bourdieu, 1990, pp. 53–55); from the biological notion of third-order autopoietic systems (Graham and Luke, 2003; Graham and McKenna, 2000; Luhmann, 1995; Maturana and Varela, 1980); from Lippmann's (1922) social theory of stereotypes; from Cooley's (1909) perspective on the 'social mind'; or from the metaphorical perspective of Wilson's (1887) 'public opinion' as the demagogue of democracy. Each of those perspectives will show up different linkages between individual and social levels of cognition and action, and each will emphasise the vastly different kinds of capacities possessed by individuals and social systems, and how those are exercised and instantiated over time, well beyond the life of any individual.

That Creel conceived of a social level of cognition is evident in the many such comments he made, such as his framing of the CPI's efforts as a 'fight for the mind of man' (1920, Ch. 8). Three aspects are essential to be taken into account when considering a perspective on social cognition when it comes to the CPI and its legacy. First, the CPI showed us how the social mind can be "scaled up" to transcend localisms and ethnic tribalisms, raising questions about the limits of social unity. Importantly, in this, the CPI campaign was largely positive, even while organised around conflict, encouraging unity along associative and identificatory lines rather than later (and earlier) negative "call-to-arms" campaigns that have relied on a scapegoat of one kind or another to provide unity of purpose (Burke, 1950/1969; Graham, Keenan, and Dowd, 2004). Second, in scaling up the social mind around a rhetoric of warfare, the CPI conducted a mass assault on memory across spatial, linguistic, ethnic, axiological, and historical lines. It had to motivate a public that had demonstrated just six months earlier that it was largely pacifist or at least neutral by voting for Wilson's 1916 election platform. It also had to achieve all that in the context of rivalrous ethno-linguistic groups, many of whom had come from opposing sides of the conflict into which they were now to be cajoled. The CPI had therefore to transcend older nationalities in the development of a new "synthetic" national identity. In triumphing over history, language, memory, and nationality, the CPI also overcame core values of a competitive commercial mindset to achieve an unprecedented level of collaboration. That leads to the third important aspect of the social cognition perspective: there is a seemingly intractable paradox at the centre of what the CPI achieved. At the start of America's engagement in WWII, Burke (1942) notes the following: 'In America we are apparently confronting the need to change from a commercial-liberal-monetary nexus of motives to a collective-sacrificial-military nexus of motives as the principle shaping the logic of the nation's effort' (p. 404). The paradox is that social minds organised around extremely competitive, self-interested commerce—so often described as a non-combative situation by people as different as Adam Smith (1776/1997), Walter Ong (1977), and Thomas Friedman (1999)—seem invariably drawn to large-scale, physically destructive violence at international levels. The pattern has been repeated time and time again. It also suggests that the systematic suppression of rhetoric—meant here as the practice of partisan, agonistic verbal debate aimed at forensic, deliberative, and pedagogic ends among, within, and between social systems—if not cause for, is at least a close companion to massive physical violence. That suggests that peace among human social systems may well be impossible, and so we must consciously choose between the kinds of "battles" we wish to engage in, between rhetorical sophistication or napalm and nuclear bombs. An understanding of motives and how they are "placed" may well be, as Kenneth Burke (1945/1962) suggests, the key to the "perfection" of war, to its de-lethalisation.

The CPI achieved the nationalisation of pragmatic rhetorical method; a rapid acceleration and consequent diffusion of rhetoric, both functionally and along the lines of different media; and a rapid refiguring of partisan rhetorical probabilities (opinions) into the clothing of scientific fact. Ong (1977) notes the parcelling out of rhetoric into various pragmatic areas, noting that 'rhetoric today has diffused itself in many forms through our culture and no longer has the neater contours of earlier, less exfoliated civilizations' (p. 16). Creel sped that process up considerably. He divided the activities of the CPI into various functions and 'divisions': 'the division of news', 'the Four Minute Men', 'history', 'film', 'pictorial publicity', 'war expositions', 'the speaking division', 'the advertising division', 'the Americanizers', 'the division of women's war-work', 'the foreign section', 'the service bureau', 'syndicate features', 'the bureau of cartoons', and 'the official bulletin' (Creel, 1920). The rhetorical work done under those headings would become what is today called, in summary, "strategic communication", which includes advertising, integrated marketing communication, public relations, public diplomacy, psychological operations, organisational communication, and propaganda. In what follows, I lay out the CPI's activities under the indicative headings set out by Creel, realising that his account is one sided and quite partial (Auerbach, 2015). I foreground various aspects of rhetoric in doing so to show, not merely the classical underpinnings of Creel's rhetoric, but to identify what were essentially new rhetorics that underpin what would later become neofeudal corporatism, a post-capitalist and global mode of organisation that relies entirely upon powerful rhetorics of identification and crisis for its functioning.

The Division of News

Creel's (1920) description of the CPI's News division includes the following: 'Everything with which we had to do was new and foreign to the democratic process. There were no standards to measure by, no trails to follow, and, as if these were not difficulties enough, the necessities of the hour commanded instant action' (p. 70). The first personnel Creel employed for News were literary hands, two of them with muckraking pedigrees, Ernest Poole of *McLure's* and Edgar Sisson, editor of Rockefeller's *Cosmopolitan*, which had by then almost a decade of experience in rhetorically focused national discourse. The third was Arthur Bullard who had published on the need to mobilise the United States only a month before the CPI came into being (Bullard, 1917). Again, Creel explains the CPI as a fact producer:

> What was needed, and what we installed, was official machinery for the preparation and release of all news bearing upon America's war effort—not opinion nor conjecture, but facts—a running record of each day's progress in order that the fathers and mothers of the United States might gain a certain sense of partnership. Newspaper men of standing and ability were sworn into the government service and placed at the very heart of endeavor in the War and Navy departments, in the War Trade Board, the War Industries Board, the Department of Justice, and the Department of Labor. It was their job to take deadwood out of the channels of information, permitting a free and continuous flow.
>
> (Creel, 1920, p. 72)

The pragmatic "facts" of news were disposed with the rhetorical end being that 'the fathers and mothers of the United States' would identify with the war effort: facts in the service of attitude. The need for a 'free and continuous flow' of facts is pure Erasmian copia and disposition. The news division long predated the post-9/11 "embedded reporter", again a means of promoting identification between reporters and that on which they are expected to report, and is most likely the first "24/7" news service, predating CNN by 63 years.

> The Division of News kept open the whole twenty-four hours. Every "story," on the moment of its completion, was mimeographed and "put on the table" in the pressroom where the news associations kept regular men, and to which the correspondents came regularly. These "stories" were "live news," meant for the telegraph wire, and the method employed assured speedy, authoritative, and equitable distribution of the decisions, activities and intentions of the government in its warmaking branches.
>
> (Creel, 1920, p. 72)

The paradoxes of Creel's rhetorical dedication to unbiased facts are exemplified in his statement that the division reported 'in exactly the same colorless style the remarkable success of the Browning guns, on the one hand, and on the other the existence of bad health conditions in three or four of the cantonments' (Creel, 1920, p. 73). The news division became the paradigm of administrative centralisation, 'the one central information bureau' that made things less costly for the newspapers and more convenient for the government, providing an ongoing account of the war effort and servicing 12,000 rural newspaper each week with a digest of galley-proofed stories (pp. 74–75).

The Four Minute Men

The rhetorical sophistication of the CPI is demonstrated by its treatment of different media forms. The Four Minute Men was a national network of speakers whose job it was to speak on centrally coordinated topics wherever people gathered in numbers, thus treating each collective event as a unique medium. Many of the speakers were trained by a professor of rhetoric from Chicago (Auerbach, 2015, p. 85). The Four Minute Men spoke at 'the meetings of lodges, fraternal organizations, and labor unions', with most speakers being selected 'from the membership of the organizations to whom they spoke'; they spoke 'at all meetings of the granges in many states'; at around 500 'lumber-camps of the country'; at 'Indian reservations'; at 'churches, synagogues, and Sunday-schools'; at 'matinee performances in the motion-picture theaters'; 'to the members of women's clubs and other similar organizations'; and at 153 colleges, and at schools across the country (p. 90). In one of Creel's rare mentions of music, there was also 'four-minute singing' at workplaces, and 'a bulletin of specially selected songs was prepared and issued. The various chairmen appointed song-leaders, to take charge of motion-picture-theater audiences, and the venture was a success from the first' (p. 93). Creel cites official figures of 755,190 speeches to a cumulative audience of 314,454,514 people in 18 months. But, he says, the real number was closer to a million speeches for a cumulative audience of over 400 million at a total cost of $101,555.10 (p. 94). Creel's description of the Four Minute Men is the description of a weapon:

> these were no haphazard talks by nondescripts, but the careful, studied, and rehearsed efforts of the *best* men in each community, each speech aimed as a rifle is aimed, and driving to its mark with the precision of a bullet. History should, and will, pay high tribute to the Four Minute Men, an organization unique in world annals, and as effective in the battle at home as was the onward rush of Pershing's heroes at St. Mihiel.
>
> (p. 94)

Again, the rhetoric is addressed, more directly than any other he describes. He notes the risks of launching 'an army of speakers . . . vested in large degree with the authority of the government' and claims that if he had more time to think it over, he may not have approved what was a largely uncontrollable talking army (pp. 84–85). There is little doubt that a rhetoric of identification with the highest authority in the land, along with the hierarchic value of being chosen among 'the best' of the community, led the participants in the Four Minute Men to subsidise the program at 90 times its funded cost.

The kinds of authoritative gravity insinuated into each speaking event can be seen in the device Creel describes for use at cinema events. A glass slide with the following was projected onto the screen prior to the speech at interval:

4 MINUTE MEN 4
(Copyright, 1917. Trade-mark.)

———————

(Insert name of speaker)
will speak four minutes on a subject of national importance.
He speaks under the authority of
THE COMMITTEE ON PUBLIC INFORMATION
GEORGE CREEL, CHAIRMAN
WASHINGTON, D.C. (Creel, 1920, p. 85)

Rather than prescribing details of speeches, the CPI used the ancient rhetorical technique of topical disposition. Creel is clear that the CPI did 'not want stereotyped oratory' and instead settled on 'regular bulletins' being issued, 'each containing a budget of material covering every phase of the question to be discussed' (p. 86). A selection of topics and their arrangement in time includes the following:

Topic	Period
Universal Service by Selective Draft.	May 12–21, 1917
First Liberty Loan	May 22–June 15, 1917
Red Cross	June 18–25, 1917
Food Conservation	July 1–14, 1917
Why We Are Fighting	July 23–Aug. 5, 1917
The Importance of Speed	Aug. 19–26, 1917
Maintaining Morals and Morale	Nov. 12–25, 1917
War Savings Stamps	Jan. 2–19, 1918
Lincoln's Gettysburg Address	Feb. 12, 1918
The Income Tax	Mar. 11–16, 1918
The Meaning of America	June 29–July 27, 1918
Where Did You Get Your Facts?	Aug. 26–Sept. 7, 1918

(Creel, 1920, p. 87)

By including in the speaking division's bulletin-only topics, timing, related material, and one or two exemplar speeches, the CPI recognises the fundamental considerations of oratory: variation in audience, language, speaker, context, and events, along with an arrangement of common topics to be articulated for a multitude of audiences gathered in a multitude of common places.

Film and Pictorial Publicity

I treat film and pictorial together because together they foreground a new kind of rhetoric that is almost purely visual and entirely spatial. Again, the change was qualitative rather than formal. Creel called the pictorial publicity division 'the battle of the fences' to refer to the CPI's refurbishing of public space with an entirely new aesthetic sensibility infused with nationalistic aims. The importance of public pictures to the CPI was that 'the printed word might not be read, people might not choose to attend meetings or to watch motion pictures, but the billboard was something that caught even the most indifferent eye' (Creel, 1920, p. 133). The standard fare of advertising would not do: 'What we wanted—what we had to have—was posters that represented the best work of the best artists—posters into which the masters of the pen and brush had poured heart and soul as well as genius' (p. 134). Creel is explicit about the novelty of what the CPI was engaged in with its pictorial efforts. It was a 'wholesale education to the country in that the division made the billboard "safe for art," the work standing out in sharp contrast to the commercial disfigurations of the past' (p. 136). The Division of Pictorial Publicity was staffed by 'painters, sculptors, designers, illustrators, and cartoonists' providing America with 'more posters than any other belligerent' (p. 134). Creel considered the posters as having universal appeal in their muteness, calling to domestic audiences 'from every hoarding like great clarions' and throughout the world 'captioned in every language' (p. 134). When writing about the pictorial division, Creel naturally drops discussion of "the facts" given the overtly hortatory function of the division's visual products exemplified by James Montgomery Flagg's "Uncle Sam" poster captioned with "I Want You for U.S. Army" (there are hundreds of examples of the posters available online—see multimedia references). What ensued was an 'inrush of new and more vivid thought' (p. 135). When talking of pictorial, Creel tends mainly to focus on the character of the artists themselves, and on the edifying qualities of art. The artists 'felt a great sense of responsibility', they were 'a harmonious unit' that 'worked together in the common cause' and 'sank personal considerations', were filled with 'a fine spirit of helpfulness', aimed for 'the highest excellence in all commissions', thereby 'stirring patriotism', and 'awakening in the public mind the importance of artists' (p. 136). It is noteworthy that Creel moves away from asserting the factual nature of the CPI's work in his discussion of the pictorial division, moving instead into praise for ethos and aesthetics.

Not so with the Division of Film, which also includes still photography as well as the moving image. Unlike Speaking and Pictorial divisions, Creel talks about the problems of film in institutional terms. Easy readings of the relationships between the CPI and Hollywood suggest that this was the first point at which the US military and Hollywood joined forces (see, e.g., Mirlees, 2016; CDI, 1997). To some extent that is true, although the path is not at all straightforward. Creel faced two major and basic issues with moving and still photography: production and distribution. The issue facing production was the need for an "army" of photographers to have access to the daily goings on both at home and abroad. Production expertise was largely commercial, especially where print was concerned, and the processes for mass printing of photographs were quite new. Add to this the relative newness of moving picture production processes, and their chaotic, new, and commercially idiosyncratic distribution, exchange, and exhibitor networks, and the rhetorical challenge becomes more about logistics and commercial politics than any established rhetorical method. Creel had to persuade an entirely new and self-obsessed industrial "scene" to get his film rhetoric done.

The movie was one of two new semi-commodities, the other being the phonograph cylinder or disk. Both the film and the record required commodities other than the text's medium to "play" the program. The moving picture required high-cost machines to be recorded and played, and the equipment, along with the movies that were shot and played on it, was strictly controlled through a web of aggressively contested patents, licenses, release and return contracts, and large and shifting combinations of companies fighting over different aspects of the industry and its business. All those aspects were the subjects of ongoing legal battles, ranging from actions about patents, to actions about anti-trust laws and restraint of trade. Distribution quickly became the point of commercial power, with an oligopoly network of major distributors having been formed by the time the CPI had launched. They included Paramount, Universal, Warners, and Pathé (Alvarez, 2005). Those major distributors had already started the move towards vertical integration, moving into production and the business of the movie exchange.

The amount of activity in the moving picture sector by 1917 was staggering by any estimate. The central motives of the activity were the shortness of the films on offer, demand for new material, and the high cost of making prints, all of which led to the need to circulate individual prints rapidly and widely. In 1908, a standard nickelodeon theatre would run up to seven one-reel (at 11 minutes or so per reel) features per day and required up to 40 reels per week to keep their schedule going. The usual number of prints made of any one film in 1908 averaged around 40 copies. By 1909, the number was 50 to 60 (Alvarez, 2005, p. 438). By 1910, Pathé had 160 prints of each release ready, with up to 350 for its most popular offerings (2005, p. 438). Those prints, and at one point the equipment to play them, were leased through networks of film exchanges whose business was sub-leasing the prints to movie exhibitors at high rates of turnover, rather like a Blockbuster video rental store for movie print exhibitors. The movement of the prints around the country was a logistic cyclone. Prints spent much of their time in transport and 'it was estimated that the U.S. film industry spent at least \$5,000,000 annually in express company charges' in 1910 alone (p. 438).

The public demand for new material was voracious, and the sector was built around it at every level. The need to get limited amounts of new prints to and from exhibitors, of which there were thousands, resulted in a time-critical ethos tied to exchange and exhibitor competition which led to the still-problematic 'release date' system. A scan of the most popular subject matter treated by movies indicates that most of the popular movie titles in the years leading up to the US involvement in the war can be categorised largely as moral fare.

For example, the top-grossing movie of 1915 was D. W. Griffith's *Birth of a Nation*, earning \$10 million. It was a three-hour feature based on a play called *The Clansman*, a racist tale praising the Ku Klux Klan and warning against the rise to power of African Americans. Griffith's work again topped the billing in 1916 with *Intolerance*, another three-hour marathon of morality tales from Babylon to Modern America that were a rebuke to critics of his previous year's film. In 1917, the top-grossing film was *Cleopatra*, a Fox movie casting the historic queen as an ambitious and 'wanton woman', thus deserving of the fate that befell her. In 1918, the top-grossing movie was a romantic comedy, *Mickey*, a variant on the *Cinderella* theme in which a 'tomboy' orphan from a mining settlement is sent to her New York aunt for some corrective feminine attention and upsets the aunt's aims for her own daughter to marry a mining magnate.

The reason for my digression into the contemporary detail of the movie sector is the way in which Creel presents the Film Division's activities and the almost total absence of historical mention of the CPI from the business end of the movie sector. In 1918, there are but a few titles of note in the trade publications—including *The Heart of Humanity*, *My Four Years in Germany* (Warner Brothers' first film), and *The Sinking of the Lusitania*—that were produced as part of US war efforts. In the main, there is barely a ripple made by the CPI in the raging torrent of movie titles that flooded American culture at the time, the success of which was the constant focus of the sector. A prominent CPI advertisement in the 1918 *Moving Picture World*, an influential independent trade publication of the era, is the two-page '*Roll of Honor in the name of every theatre which exhibits Pershing's Crusaders the first U.S. official war feature*' (*The Moving Picture World*, 1918, pp. 29–30 [italics are author's own]). The advertisement ran for six weeks in 1918 as an encouragement to exhibitors to show the film. The roll and date of its appearance attests to the long-lead time required for the CPI to enter the movie business and find ways to tap into its complex, hypercompetitive systems, and to the lengths it needed to go to garner support for exhibition. Part of the answer came in the CPI's sale of news weeklies to the movie news agencies.

Creel demonstrates his grasp of the movie distribution environment when arguing up the success of *America's Answer*:

> In the film industry a booking of 40 per cent, of the theaters is considered as 100 per cent, distribution because of the close proximity of a great number of theaters, rendering them dependent on the same patronage that is, theaters are plotted as available in zones rather than as individual theaters; thus three theaters in one zone present but one possible booking because of the identity of clientele. Taking this into consideration, the distribution of government features approximated 80 per cent, and 90 per cent, rather than 50 per cent, distribution, although on "America's Answer," in certain territories such as New York and Seattle, the percentage of total theaters booked reached over 60 per cent. and 54 per cent., respectively, which on the above basis would equal 100 per cent. distribution.

(p. 125)

However, the relatively scant commercial revenues that Creel records for film would have been considered a commercial failure in the terms of the day:

Pershing's Crusaders	$181,741.69
America's Answer	$185,144.30
Under Four Flags	$ 63,946.48
Official War Review	$334,622.35
Our Bridge of Ships	$992.41
U.S.A. Series	$13,864.98
Our Colored Fighters	$640.60
News weekly	$15,150.00
Miscellaneous sales	$56,641.58
Total sales from films	$852,744.30

Creel, 1920, (p. 125)

The entire sales of the CPI's Film Division were less than 10 per cent of the highest grossing film from 1915. The various historical arguments suggesting that Hollywood (by which is meant the US movie business and industries) is a creature of the US military based on the CPI's early involvement in the film industry must therefore be generally overstated. From the current perspective, it would appear that Hollywood bent the CPI to its ways based on its already military level of commercial logistics that had developed in the sector before the war, with competition rife at every level and from every possible direction based on popular taste and demand.

The Advertising Division

Creel (1920) saw the entire strategy of the CPI as being based in advertising. It was 'distinctly in the nature of an advertising campaign . . . shot through and through with an evangelical quality' and so the CPI turned 'instinctively to the advertising profession for advice and assistance' (p. 156). However, there were perceptual and moral barriers to the unvarnished use of advertising techniques that the CPI had to contend with. People didn't trust advertising. That resulted in what Creel described as an 'appalling waste in stupid or misapplied energy'. He thought that 'paid advertising—controlled, authoritative, driving to its mark with the precision of a rifle-ball—would have been quicker, simpler, and in the end far cheaper' than the kinds of voluntary efforts and "press agenting" that the CPI was forced into in its earliest days (pp. 156–157). The idea of 'voluntarism' had a 'glamour' that hid its costs, with Creel claiming it took '5 dollars to secure the gift of a dime' for the First Liberty Loan (p. 157). He sees the formal establishment of the CPI's Advertising Division by Wilson as an historic 'recognition of advertising as a real profession . . . and an honorable and integral part of the war-machinery of government' (p. 158).

Once again, faced with division, Creel's impulse is to engage a rhetoric of identification. Instead of aiming at a budget for straight-ahead, paid advertising, the CPI's 'Chicago Plan' consisted in soliciting donations of 1-million-dollar worth of advertising space to be 'filled with effective appeals prepared by selling experts' (Creel, 1920, p. 157). Identifying advertising with the spirit of donation helped remove it from the suspicion that clung to any suggestion of commercial benefit, an opposite strategy to that of the Film Division which required the CPI to identify with commercial interests in order that it be taken seriously by the riot of competing commercial interests involved. Like the speaking division, Creel organised advertising along existing lines of association, employing people with "connections" to coordinate the massive networks needed for mobilisation. They included

> Mr. William H. Johns, chairman, president of the American Association of Advertising Agencies, representing 115 leading firms of this kind in the country; Mr. Thomas Cusack, one of the acknowledged leaders of the poster and painted bulletin industry; Mr. W. C. D'Arcy, president of the Associated Advertising Clubs of the World, representing 180 advertising clubs with a combined membership of 17,000; Mr. O. C. Harn, chairman of the National Commission of the Associated Advertising Clubs of the World; Mr. Herbert S. Houston, formerly president of the Associated Advertising Clubs of the World; Mr. Lewis B. Jones, president of the Association of National Advertisers; and Mr. Jesse H. Neal, executive secretary of the Associated Business Papers, consisting of 500 leading trade and technical publications.
>
> (p. 158)

These were Creel's 'generals' of advertising who ran an unprecedented 'machinery that operated with . . . automatic efficiency' (p. 159). For each new issue that arose, they 'studied the problem, planned the campaign, [and] decided upon the agency best fitted to prepare the copy' (p. 159). They coordinated communication, copy, and artwork for everything from 'patriotic window displays'; to daily, weekly, and monthly publications; to 'the use of billboards and the painted sign' (p. 160). As an exemplar, Creel gives broad brushstroke on the efforts required by the division to help enlist 13 million men into the US armed forces between April 1917 and September 12, 1917:

> about two weeks were allowed to the office of the Provost-Marshal-General in which to reach every American between eighteen and forty-five with specific information and instructions. . . . Expert copywriters, working night and day, put the facts of registration in advertising form, the Division of Pictorial Publicity furnished illustrations, display experts put the product into type, and the whole was issued as an Advertising Service Bulletin and sent to every advertiser and advertising agent in the United States . . . in form ready to use, was advertising copy in any space from one column to a page, suitable to any medium from a metropolitan daily to a country weekly . . . The next publication was a Selective Service Register—a regular newspaper with one side of the sheet given over entirely to questions and answers, specific instructions, and general appeals; the other side a striking poster, blazoning the fundamental facts of registration . . .

The Division of Distribution, augmenting its force and working day and night shifts, distributed some 20,000,000 copies of the two publications to . . . 18,000 newspapers, 11,000 national advertisers and agencies, 10,000 chambers of commerce and their members, 30,000 manufacturers' associations, 22,000 labor unions, 10,000 public libraries, 32,000 banks, 58,000 general stores, 3,500 Young Men's Christian Association branches, 10,000 members of the Council of National Defense, 1,000 advertising clubs, 56,000 post-offices, 55,000 railroad station agents, 5,000 draft boards, 100,000 Red Cross organizations, 12,000 manufacturers' agents. . . . The foreign-language groups were reached by the establishment of direct contacts with 600 papers printed in nineteen different languages.

(pp. 161–162)

Creel's understanding of the Advertising Division as a form of rhetorical weaponry is evident when he says its output 'served also as ammunition for the Four Minute Men, and fifty thousand speakers backed up the printed word. Even the Division of Films was brought into the team-play' (p. 162).

He notes with pride that the CPI turned the generally mistrusted field of advertising into a respected profession. That idea that the CPI had transformed what was once a pariah occupation into a dignified profession based on its proven ability to enlist a country into the largest and most deadly war up to that point in history raises many questions that cannot be addressed here. The main themes and patterns of the CPI's work provide no further theoretical insight past those already mentioned here. There were many other approaches by the CPI made specifically for different audiences, especially foreign and domestically ethnic ones, but the rhetorical strategies held throughout: centralise and coordinate the efforts of existing networks of communication, commerce, and culture, and use them to "sell" the idea of "America" and its values, and to demonise "the hun".

Woodrow Wilson's words from the 1916 Congress of Salesmanship echo through the approach Creel took with the CPI.

This, then, my friends, is the simple message that I bring you. Lift your eyes to the horizons of business: do not look too close at the little processes with which you are concerned, but let your thoughts and your imaginations run abroad throughout the whole world, and with the inspiration of the thought that you are Americans and are meant to carry liberty and justice and the principles of humanity wherever you go, go out and sell goods that will make the world more comfortable and more happy, and convert them to the principles of America.

(Wilson, 1916)

Wilson's sensitivity to public opinion had had 30 years to become a thorough policy of worldwide saturation, what Creel called 'a vast enterprise in salesmanship, the world's greatest adventure in advertising' (1920, p. 4). The CPI set terms of "principles", "values", "liberty", "truth", "fact", "justice", "ideals", "unselfishness", "purpose", "morale", and transparency against terms of "ignorance", "prejudice", "indifference", "hate", "injustice", "lies", and "darkness and delusion", with the conflict being framed almost entirely in scientistic packaging designed to direct attention away from the sheer force of pragmatism's rhetorical substance: a rhetoric of action aimed at shaping the future, not only for the United States, but for the whole of human civilization. In the process, the CPI literally talked America into existence as a massive military power, overcame intense localism and intense ethnic rivalries, created a federal government with unprecedented levels of power, and kicked off what would become known as "the American Century". It was an astonishing feat of rhetoric.

4 Globalising Technique

This chapter traces the historical and international propagation of the CPI's influence into the present day. The Committee on Public Information (CPI) ceased operating internationally on June 30, 1919, and ended altogether on August 19. Its ongoing influence did not. The success of the CPI led to its activities being studied with great intensity up to the beginnings of WWII. That entailed and generated many new and still vibrant fields of study, not the least of which is communication studies in general. Up to that point, studies of communication had been confined to linguistics, psychology, propaganda, some rudimentary studies of advertising, and whatever had survived in the way of classical approaches to rhetoric and dialectic. The shock of what war propaganda had achieved by way of death and destruction, centralised government control, and the CPI's efforts in particular, sparked a new intellectual agenda, igniting interest in the new role that communication would need to play in mass societies. Prior to the war, massification of the United States was well underway. As we saw in Chapter 2, there were all sorts of new influences and demographic trends pointing towards nationalism and the massification of US society. The CPI took hold of those trends and organised, centralised, intensified, and accelerated them to the point at which they became weaponised. The reactions of the public, communicators, educators, business, and academia to the CPI were both long lasting and widespread. In a very real way, the CPI could be said to have invented the field of communication as a newly significant area of interest across all those domains.

Any detailed task of tracing the CPI's influence and the spread of its techniques would be a multi-volume work, and so I must take shortcuts and make caveats. I recommend Auerbach's (2015) account, which focuses on the influence of Ivy Lee and Byoir, for an excellent account up to WWII. The method of this chapter is personalised in so far as it focuses on the contributions of specific people who were part of or influenced by the CPI rather than, say, the systematic development of theory and practice across the fields of advertising, public relations, public diplomacy, organisational communication, and so on. At a certain point, after WWII and the "success" of the Nazi party's propaganda machine, matched by the efforts of the Allied Forces to counter their propaganda, the whole system became self-promoting.

The people I focus on here are in some ways 'characters' in the manner that Burke (1966) meant the term. They are shorthand for certain ways of seeing the world. The cast has some well-known figures, such as Walter Lippmann (1922), who ought to be considered as having founded the entire field of communication research and is probably the single most influential philosopher of communication in the 20th century, despite being largely forgotten or swept aside through misreadings or conscious elisions (Auerbach, 2015; Jansen, 2012); George Gallup, whose opinion polling service continues into the present day and whose name is synonymous with statistical public survey methods (Gallup, 2016); Edward Bernays (1928, 1923), known worldwide (and incorrectly) as "the father of Public Relations'" (Auerbach, 2015); Harold Lasswell (1972, 1941, 1938, 1927), who by 1941 had defined in technical terms the "departments" of communication research for the remainder of the 20th century; and Paul Lazarsfeld (1940) whose empirical studies of radio audience responses largely shaped the methods and assumptions of empirical sociology into the current era. There are also villains, such as Goebbels, Mussolini, and Stalin, and lesser known characters, too, such as S. I. Hayakawa (1941, 1939), Ivy Lee, Carl Byoir, and Clyde Miller of the Institute for Propaganda Analysis. The list might well include many others, such as Theodor Adorno and the many critical scholars up to those of the present day whose work has focused on the manipulation of mass perceptions, but for whom space and purpose do not permit discussion here. In the global spread of the CPI's techniques, the overarching theme and backdrop is "national" strategy in the classic sense of the word that implies an enemy to be beaten.

Walter Lippmann

Walter Lippmann set the ambivalent tone for post-war communication studies in 1922 with his *Public Opinion*, which James Carey rightly calls 'the originating book in the modern history of communication research' (1997, p. 22). Lippmann is generally critical of the CPI's efforts, although his criticisms were aimed at the CPI's effectiveness and execution rather than its intent. He was especially scathing of Creel's censorship. In some accounts (e.g., Mirlees, 2016) Lippmann is included as a member of the CPI, but that is incorrect (Auerbach, 2015, p. 94; Jansen, 2012, pp. 75–79). Lippmann reacted to the CPI by developing a sophisticated, critical theory of symbolism to comprehend the functioning of public opinion, and proceeds from the view that war is a unique and exemplary case when it comes to understanding the organisation of human interests and actions.

He recognised that war is a very special kind of cooperation and requires total involvement in a symbolic milieu based on hatred, or perhaps love, depending on which way you see it (cf. Burke, 1945/1962). The same principles cannot be applied in peace time because people's interests turn inwards and become fragmented. His experience during the war led him to see that societies had become connected in new ways that relied on new kinds of "shorthands" for comprehending distant realities which might affect their lives at some point, but which were at the same time incomprehensible and quite possibly irrelevant. Those shorthands were based on 'fictions' to which people responded, despite their almost total ignorance of either the veracity or importance of any given issue, or the people involved in it. He called those fictions 'stereotypes', and it is his best remembered contribution to communication theory (Lippmann, 1922, Ch. 6)

Lippmann's stereotypes are idiomatic networks of symbolic shorthand that each of us uses based on our immersion in a unique blend of artistic, cultural, political, business, and social environments. We necessarily use stereotypes to classify people, trends, situations, and events because reality is too overwhelmingly complex for us to go to the effort of registering and classifying things anew each time we encounter them. He therefore sees stereotyping as inevitable based on its relative psychic 'economy', but is concerned to warn against taking our stereotypes too seriously. His stereotypical "cure", what he calls variously 'inoculation' and 'antiseptic', is a critical philosophy recognising that each person 'is only a small part of the world' and therefore understands 'only phases and aspects' of the world through what is 'a coarse net of ideas' peculiar to each individual. With such a philosophy to hand, he says, 'when we use our stereotypes, we tend to know that they are only stereotypes, to hold them lightly, to modify them gladly' (pp. 90–91).

Lippmann's many other contributions to communication theory are generally left to the side, but among them we can number the elements of what Kenneth Burke would later call a 'rhetoric of identification' (1950/1969), 'trained incapacity' (1937/1984), and 'symbolic action' (1966); the notion of 'audience labour', the implications of which would have to wait almost six decades to be fleshed out by Dallas Smythe (1981); speech act theory, later to be developed by J. L. Austin (1962); the attention economy; the understanding that different moods entail different kinds of reasoning; and the understanding that in the determination of "self-interest", that both "self" and "interest" are conventional constructs, and so we are often shocked to see other people acting against what we might assume to be their best interests (Burke, 1935/1984, p. 98). Sue Curry Jansen (2012) also notes Lippmann's contributions to social epistemology, his 'fractal-like' sociology, concepts of cultural and linguistic capital, the earliest content analysis of news, the agenda setting function of news, cognitive dissonance and other consistency theories, and theories of intersubjectivity.

Lippmann is often portrayed today as an 'anti-democratic elitist' with megalomaniacal tendencies (Schudson, 2008, p. 1033; cf. Carey, 1989, 1997, pp. 22–23; Seyb, 2015). While this is not the place for a rehabilitation, I agree with Auerbach (2015), Jansen (2013, 2012, 2009), and Schudson (2008) that such a view is a complete misreading of Lippmann. *Public Opinion* is rife with disillusionment about the failures of expertise, the role of the war in undermining many Progressive Era policy achievements through censorship and the privatisation of political communication, the lack of moral conviction with which journalism responded to the CPI, and the effects of a propaganda campaign that made any reasonable and lasting peace impossible, while simultaneously losing any trust the public had for journalism. Lippmann also makes many contributions to philosophy that have gone largely unremarked, not the least of which is his subtle but profound rewriting of Peirce's philosophy of perception. Peirce argues that first we perceive, then we classify, then we judge. Lippmann argues convincingly that we start with a framework of classification (our pattern of stereotypes) and *then* we see. But because our patterns of stereotypes are so deeply grounded in feeling and context, the way we feel at any given time, combined with the social situation we are in, shapes which patterns of stereotypes we use and therefore how we classify, and our framework of classification shapes what we can see. At this point, Peirce's theory is entirely upended, and it is our emotional frame, our ever-changing feeling towards the world at large, and our social situatedness that shape our perceptual frame and therefore ultimately *what* we perceive.

Lippmann's theory of symbols is worth elaborating for its uniquely ambiguous nature, and because it underpins that most quotable and quoted term of his, 'the manufacture of consent', which has been used time and time again by pundits and critics ever since. It is a concept that deeply influenced Bernays, who along with Carl Byoir and Ivy Lee would spread the CPI's techniques to Fascist Italy, Nazi Germany, Soviet Russia, and onwards through corporate practices across the entire globe. Lippmann's theory of symbols also clearly informs Lasswell and many others, including, the symbolic interactionism of Blumer, Park, and Merton. Lippmann defines symbols as having 'transcendent practical importance', a definition that only an American steeped in Santayana's peculiar pragmatism could formulate. Symbols 'conserve unity', they are constant in human societies, 'from the totem pole to the national flag, from the wooden idol to God the Invisible King, from the magic word to some diluted version of Adam Smith or Bentham' (p. 234). They are 'focal points' where class and interest based conflicts are merged. It is a critical conception of symbolism as action and is focused on a critique of the abuse of public power.

While much has been made of Lippmann's phrase, 'manufacture of consent', which he incidentally pairs with 'creation of consent', in context, it is a very minor and summary statement of his view on public opinion as a tool of administrators to elicit either good or bad outcomes. It was not a prescription, but the observation of another major paradox associated with mass persuasion that became evident with the post-war shock at the devastation such persuasions had wrought. Suddenly persuasion had become 'a self conscious art and a regular organ of popular government' (p. 248). Lippmann is clear that neither he nor anyone else can begin to understand the consequences of the fact that 'the old constants of our thinking have become variables' in the scientific calculations of political problems (p. 248).

Lippmann objected to Creel's handling of the CPI's tasks, describing it as bombastic, insensitive, and ham fisted in understanding foreign audiences. He is known to have anonymously criticised Creel during his muckraking years and complained to Woodrow Wilson during the war about the choice of Creel for the CPI Directorship (Auerbach, 2015; Jansen, 2012). He set up a separate propaganda branch inside the army with the aim of rectifying the damage he perceived Creel to be doing in Europe. He was also intimately involved as part of "The Inquiry" in drafting Wilson's Fourteen Points, the document outlining "peace terms" for an Allied victory on which the Allied governments would all eventually agree. The famous document was a response to the moral crisis which struck among soldiers in late 1917 after a large-scale Russian defeat. It was thus an exercise by Wilson, Lippmann, and others in a rhetoric of unity on an international scale. Its audacity is breathtaking. Its aim was moral sustenance and lasting peace. It referred to an ideal future and was therefore Utopian. As such, so long as it was set in 'that hazy and happy future when the agony was to be over', the issues of competing interests and interpretations were never at issue so long as the Points 'were plans for the settlement of a wholly invisible environment' and offered hope of a peaceful and globally united future (p. 215). The document would ultimately fail to bring about the desired peace, but it brought into existence the League of Nations and eventually the United Nations. For that reason alone, as a rhetoric of identification, the Fourteen Points is unequalled for scope and reach in the history of humanity.

Bernays

Edward Bernays is probably the best known and most obviously influential member of the CPI. If anything, his view is the one that Lippmann is most often charged with having, namely that mass society *should* be run by elites. His 1928 *Propaganda* verges on manifesto and has two main aims: 'to explain the mechanism which controls the public mind' and 'to find the due place in the modern democratic scheme for this new propaganda and . . . suggest its gradually evolving code of ethics and practice' (1928/2005, p. 45). Bernays' work is recognised as being heavily influenced by Lippmann, and he is quite explicit about the point (1923, 1928, p. 71).

He views peace time propaganda as the 'new propaganda' and therefore as a new science with a 'new technique' that is underpinned by a concept of 'the mass mind' and the individual's relationship with "it" (p. 55). The 'new technique'

> takes account not merely of the individual, nor even of the mass mind alone, but also and especially of the anatomy of society, with its interlocking group formations and loyalties. It sees the individual not only as a cell in the social organism but as a cell organized into the social unit. Touch a nerve at a sensitive spot and you get an automatic response from certain specific members of the organism.
>
> (p. 55)

Bernays' public opinion is a Leviathan of minds. He is unabashedly positive that propaganda is necessary to the operation of the group mind and a force for good. His theorisation of how propaganda works in mass society is best viewed as networks of what would later be called by Lazarsfeld and Merton 'opinion leaders' (Whitman, 1991), a concept he undoubtedly owes to Lippmann (Jansen, 2012, 2013). Bernays' method is based on the assumption that 'if you can influence the leaders . . . you automatically influence the group they sway' (p. 73). He names such networks of influence variously as 'invisible government', 'invisible wire pullers', 'invisible rulers', 'the invisible cabinet', and sees them as a kind of social environment through which public opinion is constantly produced (pp. 60–65). Underneath his approach is the notion that our judgements are almost never our own; rather, they are a function of the group mind, a 'mélange of impressions' that 'unconsciously control' decisions made by any individual (p. 73). The group mind does not "think" as such. Instead 'it has impulses, habits, and emotions', and in making up its mind on any particular question, 'its first impulse is to follow the example of a trusted leader' (p. 73).

Bernays is, as Mark Crispin Miller says, 'a propagandist for propaganda' (2005, p. 17). He is concerned to register public relations among the most distinguished professions, such as law and medicine, and so espouses a similar code of ethics (p. 69). The 'public relations counsel' advises clients 'very much as a lawyer does', pleading in 'the court of public opinion' of which the public relations counsel is also 'judge and jury' (p. 64–69). Hence they must hold themselves to high standards. Bernays is clear that public relations is not advertising and that 'his work and that of the advertising agency do not overlap' (p. 65). It is instead on a par with journalism and closely allied to it and must maintain the same standards as news (p. 70).

In Bernays, we can clearly see the establishment of modern rhetorical departmentalisation, or what would later come to be called "market segmentation", that began with Creel's segmentation of both US and international audiences, parcelling out rhetorical aims with the right "packaging" for each audience. Mass society and mass industry have brought with them a new problem: the need to produce customers (p. 84). Thus the business of any given business is no longer 'confined to the manufacture and sale of a given product, but the selling of itself and of all those things for which it stands in the public mind' (p. 83). Business had also come to recognise that when an advertiser makes claims for a particular product, such as a particular brand of soap, 'it is attempting to change the public's mode of thinking' about the whole class of products with which it is in competition, 'a thing of grave importance to the whole industry' (p. 85). Therefore, each business 'must express itself and its entire corporate existence' and 'dramatize its personality and interpret its objectives in every particular in which it comes in contact with the community (or the nation) of which it is a part' (p. 85). Each business becomes a character with clearly identifiable attributes that must be articulated throughout its every aspect. Bernays here announces the birth of "branding" theory.

Bernays departmentalises public relations for various sectors: business, politics, women's activities, education, social services, and arts and science. Each sector is faced with a different problem in relation to the social mind. Bernays is a corporatist through and through. Politics is 'the first big business in America'; it is the democratic paradox of leading a nation while simultaneously serving it. He complains that politics is too much 'ballyhoo', 'all sideshows, all honors, all bombast, glitter, and speeches' (p. 111). None of this is related to the 'main business', which is for Bernays 'studying the public scientifically, . . . supplying the public with party, candidate, platform, and performance, and selling the public these ideas and products' (p. 111). He laments that while business has learned its techniques from government (by which he means the CPI), politics refuses to learn 'very much from business methods of mass distribution of ideas and products' (p. 111). He thinks political leaders should set the agenda to lead and mould the public mind to its agenda. Policy should be sold, both at home and to the world at large, by every means possible.

He sees women's groups as having the very best in propaganda techniques. He slates this to the warlike nature of the suffragette movement, to a high level of secretarial involvement in that movement, and of the high levels of cross-pollenation of personnel between the suffragette movement and the propaganda organisations of the CPI (pp. 130–131). Bernays argues it is not surprising that 'the newest weapons of persuasion' should come from the newest entrants to the political field (p. 131). Women are to be specialists in the 'new ideas and new methods of political and social house-keeping', focusing their 'organized efforts on those objects that men are likely to ignore', such as education, the arts, music clubs, cooking instruction, serving milk in schools, and so forth (p. 133).

The means of propaganda are constantly changing, and the professional must take note. In the late 19th century, 'the public meeting was the propaganda instrument par excellence' (p. 161). By 1928, it was an anachronism because of new technologies: 'the automobile takes them away from home, the radio keeps them in the home' (p. 161). The theme for Bernays in regards to media is a variant of "Sutton's Law": the propagandist has to go to where the people are. Propaganda is parasitic upon dominant social practices, specifically in terms of where people gather or are "gathered" in some form of communion through different media forms. Instruments of propaganda must conform to the standards of the medium being deployed. I define this in Chapter 6 as genre parasitism, a practice the CPI industrialised. For example, if the propagandist is to use a newspaper, they must realise that the editor will not ask 'whether a given item is propaganda or not. What is important is that it be news' (p. 163). The same goes for magazines, which are arranged topically along lines of 'health, English gardens', 'fashionable menswear', or 'Nietzschean philosophy' (p. 164). The uses for propaganda also extend to the owners of media organisations. For example, the radio in 1928 was beginning to show itself as an important advertising medium as more people became owners of radio receivers, threatening the advertising revenues of newspapers. Bernays suggested that newspapers might 'sell schedules of advertising space on the air and on the paper', pre-empting the full-service advertising agencies of the future (p. 165). In any case, the propagandist must adapt to the changes in the media landscape. Bernays sees the motion picture as 'the greatest unconscious carrier of propaganda in the world' of the late 1920s. That is because it is a market-driven medium and consequently must 'reflect, emphasize, and even exaggerate broad popular tendencies' (p. 166). Above all else, the main tool of the propagandist is 'the personality', and he argues that 'the vivid dramatization of personality will always remain one of the functions of the public relations counsel' (p. 166).

Bernays is credited (if that is the right word) with being a primary influence on Goebbels' conduct of the Nazi government's propaganda campaign. However, as Jonathan Auerbach (2015) shows, there is a far more compelling case to be made that Ivy Lee and Carl Byoir were far more influential in the spread of CPI techniques to Nazi Germany. Lee was not employed by the CPI, but he led the Red Cross' program during the war (see below). Byoir was what would be called today the CPI's Chief Operations Officer (Auerbach, Ch. 6). Both had involvements with Nazi institutions, with Byoir being hired by the Nazi government to promote the ideals of Nazism to the United States (2015, Ch. 6). Historical recriminations aside, it is an undoubted fact that both Goebbels and Hitler were pointedly aware the United States had won the propaganda war in WWI and that public opinion had become the most important front at a time when the radio was gathering force. After his failed attempt to seize power in 1923, Hitler summarised his central problem: 'Propaganda, propaganda, propaganda. All that matters is propaganda' (Hitler, 1923, cited in Taylor, 2003, p. 241). The CPI was also an overt influence in Mussolini's approach to propaganda (Rosselini, 2008). It is also well recorded as being influential in India, China, South America, and Russia. Although there was eventual discord between the United States and Russia, there was close cooperation between the two in spreading US and Russian propaganda 'behind enemy lines' in Germany (Fike, 1959, p. 100). The Red Cross also had a surprising role in proliferating the CPI's methods in Russia. Under William Boyce Thompson, a mining and finance magnate, the Red Cross set up familiar sounding organisations with names like Committee on Civic Education, the Breshkovsky Civic Committee, and the All-Russian Democratic Conference, all of which were to achieve what is now called "plausible deniability" for Thompson to act in lieu of the then US Ambassador to Russia who was seen by the Wilson administration as being ineffective (Fike, 1959, pp. 101–102).

Lasswell

Harold Lasswell is foremost of the second-generation CPI theorists, by which I mean those whose theoretical frame came from studying the CPI rather than having direct personal involvement with it. Laswell defined the boundaries for all communication studies to come, internet studies included, with his model of communication: 'Who says what in which channel to whom with what effect?'

> The scientific study of the process of communication tends to concentrate upon one or another of these questions. Scholars who study the "who," the communicator, look into the factors that initiate and guide the act of communication. We call this subdivision of the field of research control analysis. Specialists who focus upon the "says what" engage in content analysis. Those who look primarily at the radio, press, film, and other channels of communication are doing media analysis

(p. 84). When the principal concern is with the persons reached by the media, we speak of audience analysis. If the question is the impact upon audiences, the problem is effect analysis.

(1948/1960, p. 84)

Lasswell defines the entirety of communication studies in the broadest terms while simultaneously departmentalising the field. His model comes after WWII, but his influence on the field begins with a reading of Lippmann augmented by an anthropological definition of attitudes, values, and a refutation of the social mind as conceived by pragmatist philosophers.

For Lasswell (1927), the study of political communication and the study of propaganda are identical. He says that democracy is 'the dictatorship of palaver, and the technique of dictating to the dictator is named propaganda'. Propaganda is necessary for political organisation in mass society. He defines propaganda as 'the management of collective attitudes by the manipulation of significant symbols' (p. 627). Significant symbols are 'paraphernalia employed in expressing the attitudes', whether 'primitive gestures of the face and body, or more sophisticated gestures of the pen and voice' (p. 627). By 'attitude' he means 'a tendency to act according to certain patterns of valuation' (p. 627). There is such thing as a 'collective attitude', but it has nothing to do with 'a super-organic, extranatural entity', according to Lasswell, and the introduction of such a concept into the study of communication has caused much confusion by the lack of a term to describe what the anthropologists call 'a pattern'; 'the standard uniformities of conduct at a given time and place' (p. 628). Lasswell gives a passing nod to rhetoric when he distinguishes between the 'deliberative attitude' and 'the propagandist attitude', noting that while 'the most subtle propaganda closely resembles disinterested deliberation, there is no difficulty in distinguishing the extremes' (p. 628). There are many types of propaganda, definable in terms of their aims, who conducts them, their relative permanence, and whether they are directed internally or externally to groups (p. 629). Propaganda can also be categorised according to 'the object toward which it is proposed to modify or crystallize an attitude' (p. 629). Lasswell comes close to Aristotle's definition of rhetoric when he says '[w]hatever form of words helps to ignite the imagination of the practical manipulator of attitudes is the most valuable one' (p. 631). The identity, or at least clear intersection, of the "best available means" of Aristotle's rhetoric and the "whatever works" of pragmatism are in full evidence here. The "multimodality" of rhetorical means is already well understood from the CPI's efforts, and Lasswell notes that however the 'significant symbols are embodied to reach the public may be spoken, written, pictorial, or musical, and the number of stimulus carriers is infinite' (p. 631). And while Lasswell rejects any notion of a supra-individual level of cognition, he is wholly social and cultural in his understanding, anticipating Carey's (1989) ritual view of communication by decades.

Like Bernays, Lasswell is clear on the role of opinion leaders, which he terms outright as an 'elite' in 1939.

> For the scientific analysis of politics, it is useful to define the study of politics as the analysis of influence and the influential. By the term "influence" is meant control over values. . . . Those who control the most [values] are elite. In the Soviet Union the elite of the government is identical with the elite of the state; but in the United States there are important non-governmental elites of party, business, and church. Political management is concerned with retaining and extending control over values by the manipulation of the environment. Thus elites manipulate symbols, goods and services, instruments of violence, and institutional practices; they engage in propaganda, inducement, coercion, and organization.
>
> (Lasswell, 1938, pp. 7–8)

This is perhaps the earliest example of an emergent political economy of communication. While Adams (1902) linked "publicity" for the largest businesses, at which time meant "transparency" in contemporary terms, to the general welfare of the body politic, his political economic discussions are limited to a kind of public "need to know" because of how large and economically important the trusts and corporations had become. He does not, as Lasswell does here, link the symbols of propaganda with the symbols of status, goods and services, and the means of violence. Lasswell thus stands half way between what might usefully be termed the rhetorical social scientism of pragmatics and the clinical individualist scientism of the behaviourists, beginning with Watson and continuing through to the analysts of "big data" generated by 3.5 billion people connected to the internet. While rejecting a social level of cognition, Lasswell argues that individuals are conditioned by the cultural patterns in which they are embedded and in which they have an interest in defending. That is the level at which propaganda operates. His 'stimuli', 'responses', and 'suggestions' refer to 'cultural material with a recognizable meaning', and he shows that the 'strategy of propaganda' can be described fruitfully either in terms of behaviourism or anthropology (pp. 630–631).

Looking back at his early years from 1972, Lasswell is clearly aware of his central position in what would become communication research:

> When I first became acquainted with the field of public opinion and communications research there was no Roper, no Gallup, no Cantril, no Stouffer, no Hovland. Lazarsfeld was neither a person, nor a measuring

unit; or even a category. There was no survey research, content analysis, or quantified depth analysis; no computerized systems of storage, retrieval, and utilization; no inter-university networks of cooperation; no training institutes, research bureaus, professional bibliographies, magazines, or associations. So far as that goes, there was practically no radio or television broadcasting, no instant photography, either in black or in color; and no sonar, radar, infrared or laser.

(1972, p. 301)

This piece on the relationship between propaganda, which he now calls 'communication research', and policy 'clients' is extraordinary for the structure at its centre, which lays out the steps for planning and making legislative decisions. It is Cicero for the 20th century. He begins with *intelligence* (Invention, discovery of relevant facts); *prescribing* (Disposition, the arrangement and placement of actions and actors in relation to the decision); *invoking* (Enunciation or instantiation of the policy, as in a police arrest); *application* (Performance, the running through of the entire legislative process from beginning to end); and *termination* (Conclusion of the process or repeal of the decision). The "steps" or phases Lasswell outlines, after almost 50 years at the centre of developments in communication research, including his contributions to WWII, are the functional offices of Ciceronian oratory named differently and updated in character for a mass, bureaucratised, democratic society.

Lazarsfeld

Lazarsfeld belongs to the age of radio and was the first theorist of instantaneous mass communication. His methods were mixed, as was his theoretical frame, though he remained a committed individualist. His early work comparing print and radio was concerned with the question of whether radio was culturally uplifting for those without the literacy to access print, whether people were actually inclined to listen to "serious" programming, which he defines explicitly in terms of high and low culture, and most importantly, he asks why that is the case (Lazarsfeld, 1940). He notes with some circularity that literacy is tied to economic status and that " 'more serious reading, the content of which is defined by high culture, can be expected from the better educated. In fact the 'neighborhood in which they live is an index of what they read'" (1940, pp. 12–13). Lazarsfeld set out to test three general questions: first the question about 'a feeling that radio, in general, reaches people who do not read', which proved to be the case, with people who read less listen to radio more than their bookish compatriots (p. 15). The second question was whether '*people of low cultural level listen to serious broadcasts*' (p. 14). Again, the problem of ordering culture from high to low runs into circularities about quality, seriousness, and so on. His third question is to ask why people like certain programs, again with some semantic difficulties in ordering programs, probably inevitable in any investigation of meaning.

But aside from that, Lazarsfeld's 1940 studies are of impressive mass and rigour, even today. They are almost totally scientistic despite their qualitative elements, and their efforts to identify motives are oriented toward the improvement of literacy in general. Lazarsfeld is the first to suggest the ideas of what would later be termed 'multiliteracies' (New London Group, 1996):

> The United States points with pride to its small and declining illiteracy rate. But at the same time science makes such rapid progress that the proportion of what a person does not know to what he knows is probably much greater nowadays than it was when very few knew how to write or to read. In fact, if literacy is defined as competence to understand the problems confronting us, there is ground for suggesting that we are becoming progressively illiterate today in handling life's options. And since it is no longer possible to make major decisions in local town meetings, the future of democracy depends upon whether we can find new ways for the formation and expression of public will without impairing our democratic form of government.
>
> (Lazarsfeld, 1940, pp. xi–xii)

As a Viennese escaped from Hitler, Lazarsfeld is understandably concerned about the state of democracy in the face of radio and situates improvements for democracy as his main motivation. Yet like Gallup, and even Bernays, Lazarsfeld seems somewhat naïvely to believe that once opinions, preferences, and motivations are known, the government will respond in accordance with them, even while showing how opinions are manufactured.

Crimes and Criticisms

Even criticisms of the CPI served to proliferate its effects throughout the humanities and social sciences, and throughout corporate and political spheres, worldwide. Post-war reactions to the CPI were as mixed as they were divisive. On the one side were those like George Gallup (1938), who thought public opinion research would revolutionise government, business, and society. In hyping direct mass democracy, Gallup, echoing James Bryce, claimed that 'the final stage in our democracy would be reached if the will of the majority of citizens were to become ascertainable at all times'

(1938, p. 9). His Institute of Public Opinion 'conducted a continuous day-by-day, week-by-week census of the public mind' for two years in order to achieve the aim (p. 9). Issues were of course decided in advance, and so the aim of Bryce to govern 'without the need of voting machinery at all' was undercut by the semantic limitations of issue framing.

To S. I. Hayakawa (1939) and others such as Clyde Miller and his colleagues in the Institute for Propaganda Analysis (Hobbs and McGee, 2014), the very concept of public manipulation, or any efforts at communication that relied upon "distortions" of truth and clarity, were the worst social evils. Like Plato and his intellectual descendants, they sought a public educated in the virtues of "neutral" vocabulary rather than a rhetorical solution to problems of opinion (Hayakawa, 1941). Brown (1937) notes the heated conflict about issues of nationalism and internationalism leading up to the WWII, with the utopianists of the day arguing that radio would bring 'Peace on Earth', while others argued that it would undoubtedly lead to a hot, competitive nationalism. Hitler was already in the German Chancellery. Orson Welles' *War of the Worlds* hoax would happen within months, irritating general concerns about the new medium (Hobbs and McGee, 2014). Brown is vaguely reminiscent of Lippmann when he talks about the nature of second-hand knowledge of international institutions, such as the League of Nations, in relation to the symbols of nationalism and their role in shaping the 'public mind' (p. 324). He is concerned that thought becomes

> emotionalized and . . . directed by irrational motives rather than the intellect. . . . A flag becomes holier than a human life and a symbol greater than that for which it stands, while the youth of a nation are but marionettes, dancing to their death.
>
> (p. 324)

The spread of fascism in Europe was regarded with mixed reaction in the United States and other Anglophile countries. Hitler's success with the radio was noted only in passing by Hayakawa who uses him to exemplify what he calls 'two-valued orientation' (1941, pp. 130–131), a term that would today be rendered as 'binary' or 'Manichean' (Kellner, 2004). Until the atrocities of Nazism and Fascism had become widely known, Hitler, Mussolini, and the various fascisms that had broken out worldwide were regarded as respectable in many circles, especially in military and corporate sectors. That was so much the case that the New Deal was run by a US enthusiast of fascism who later became an embarrassment to the government, resigning after Mussolini had proven belligerent (Whitman, 1991). Byoir and Lee would go to work for the Nazi party (Auerbach, 2015), and Alfred Sloan, CEO of General Motors and cornerstone of contemporary management theory, along with Henry Ford, aided the Nazi war efforts, with Sloan staying on the board of Opel throughout WWII.

The Ford corporation also did well from Nazi aggression. Hitler was said to keep a picture of Henry Ford on his wall. While the company denied it had any control over its factories in Germany following the start of the war, research in the US National Archival documents found during a Jewish reparations case in 1998 show that 'German Ford served as an "arsenal of Nazism" with the consent of headquarters in Dearborn', a fact that was officially reported in 1945 (Silverstein, 2000). The company kept ties with Nazi Germany through its operations in France, and in 1938, Henry Ford 'accepted the Grand Cross of the German Eagle, the Nazi regime's highest honor for foreigners' (Silverstein, 2000).

The national industrial plans of Stalinist Russia (five-year plans) and Fascist Germany (four-year plans) were based on Taylor's scientific management system, just as they were throughout the West following the Great Depression of the early 1930s (Shearer, 1996, p. 158; Merkle, 1980, pp. 200–202). Henry Ford and Stalin shared the services of Albert Kahn, an industrial architect who designed and built factories for both, but refused to work for Hitler. Massive expenditures on public infrastructure led to the usual public suspicions, justified and otherwise, of all the issues the muckrakers had dealt with years before. Chester Barnard, a 1930s' management expert from the Bell Telephone Company, outlined the imperatives for 'administrative management' of the nation based on imperatives for efficiency. He was sure that government could and should be run along the same lines as business. It would require a centralised approach with an acute sensitivity to communication, transparency, and clear communication of objectives. The application of corporate management principles to government had been a long time in development, beginning with Taylor's 1911 address to Congress. Barnard's contribution marks the date at which the full marriage of scientific understandings of management, communication, organisation, and political administration are fused.

Barnard developed a totally scientistic definition of organisation reminiscent of Taylor 'from which persons as well as physical and social environments are excluded as components' (Barnard, 1938, p. 72). That would allow the same system to apply to all areas of society, whether to 'a military, a religious, an academic, a manufacturing, or a fraternal' organisation (p. 65). A central concern for any organisation must be

> material progress . . . an important basis of the characteristic forms of modern western organization . . . which consists in the cult of science as a means to material ends . . . and in its more obvious current forms it consists in extensive and intensive salesmanship, advertising,

and propaganda concerning the satisfactions to be had from the use of material products.

(p. 151)

Communication would thereafter be central to management theory, strategy, and practice, and would form part of corporate, government, and all forms of human organisation from that point onwards (Dixon, 1996).

National Spectacle and the Arts of Mass Confusion

Josef Goebbels was without doubt a genius of propaganda. His approach to propaganda is revolutionary for its integration of technology, culture, history, architecture, and all forms of art. Facts would be what he said they were. He understood that deep emotion lay at the heart of successful propaganda and that all and any media forms could be infused with the emotions necessary to the organisation of mass attitudes (Bullock, 1991, p. 440). Goebbels' achievements as a propagandist are legion, but his emphasis on art and emotion is historically new. He went well beyond Creel's dedication to the organisation of factual matter to aim at an overwhelmingly emotional engagement of the German people. He managed to build an hysterical cult of hero worship to a degree that was unique up to that point in history and would not be repeated until Beatlemania in the 1960s.

By the end of WWII, propaganda and counterpropaganda techniques had been worked out on all sides of the conflict. They had become self-promoting. Organisers of war would move into private enterprise and take the techniques for organising war and war propaganda with them. Private enterprise would continue to influence a continually weakened state, both through the "revolving door" mechanism and through the mass employment of "consultants". Combined with scientific management of organisations, and the rise of new communication technologies that gave international corporations facility to organise on a global scale, the finely honed propaganda techniques developed for campaigns of mass destruction would now be fought against in grade school during media literacy lessons (New London Group, 2010); in popular critiques such as those by Hermann and Chomsky, Pilger, and Moore; or in less accessible parts of the academy focused on critical studies of mass media and communication.[1] Long-range air transport demonstrated it could traverse the globe non-stop by 1957, in an airborne repeat of Roosevelt's "Great White Fleet", "sending a message" that the United States could drop nuclear ordnance anywhere in the world. Every such move thereafter would "send a message" in response.

In 1961, communication went extra-terrestrial with the launch of Telstar, and the "space race" began as part of a decades-long Cold War in which published numbers of nuclear weapons, the goods available to the average citizen under each system, belligerent posturings such as the Bay of Pigs incident, and wars of political ideology such as those waged in Korea and Vietnam were all part of an ongoing international propaganda campaign. Each belligerent act, each technological achievement, and each social failure became part of a calculated system of "sending a message" from one side to the other. War would become "branded". Jonathan Auerbach notes that the PR firm that absorbed Carl Byoir's firm, Hill and Knowlton, was paid $12 million to promote the 1990 US-led invasion of Iraq (2015, p. 165).

In 2001, radical Islam "sent a message" to the West in the form of an attack on the World Trade Centre and the Pentagon. By 2013, following 12 years of serial wars purportedly waged in response to radical Islam's propaganda, with hundreds of millions spent on advertising and public relations consultants in Iraq, Afghanistan, Syria, and many other places, it was clear that the rhetorical techniques that had been honed for a century were simply not working any more.

> The U.S. Government has for many years been encouraged by large contractors to approach communications objectives through techniques heavily influenced by advertising and marketing. These techniques attempt to change hostile attitudes to the United States and its foreign policy in the belief that this will subsequently reduce hostile behavior . . . while an attitudinal approach may work in convincing U.S. citizens to buy consumer products, it does not easily translate to the conflict- and crisis-riven societies to which it has been applied.
>
> (Tatham, 2013, p. xiii)

The world had gotten "media savvy". The faithful techniques had stopped working.

In 1989 the Russian Soviet system failed and the Berlin Wall came down. In its wake, the USSR fragmented into its component states, and Russia was dominated by a series of 'experiments' including 'perestroika, which led to liberal euphoria, economic disaster, oligarchy, and the mafia state' (Pomerantsev, 2014). Enter Vladislav Surkov, with degrees in Theatre and Economics, who has held portfolios at the Kremlin in 'ideology, media, political parties, religion, modernization, innovation, foreign relations, and . . . modern art' (Pomerantsev, 2014). He is perhaps the first to use a new propaganda system called various names, including "hypernormalisation" and "Oh Dearism" (Curtis, 2016). Its basis is blatant contradiction.

> Surkov has directed Russian society like one great reality show. He claps once and a new political party appears. He claps again and creates Nashi, the Russian equivalent of the Hitler Youth, who are trained for street battles with potential pro-democracy supporters and burn books

by unpatriotic writers on Red Square. As deputy head of the administration he would meet once a week with the heads of the television channels in his Kremlin office, instructing them on whom to attack and whom to defend, who is allowed on TV and who is banned, how the president is to be presented, and the very language and categories the country thinks and feels in. Russia's Ostankino TV presenters, instructed by Surkov, pluck a theme (oligarchs, America, the Middle East) and speak for 20 minutes, hinting, nudging, winking, insinuating, though rarely ever saying anything directly, repeating words like "them" and "the enemy" endlessly until they are imprinted on the mind.

(Pomerantsev, 2014)

Adam Curtis (2016) gives evidence that Surkov's methods are in use by the UK government. They amount to a form of Orwellian 'doublespeak' and are the exact opposite of Creel and the CPI: where Creel aimed at unity, Surkov aims at fragmentation; where Creel claimed to aim at facts and clarity, Surkov aims at confusion and misdirection; where Creel aimed at singularity of purpose, Surkov aims to promote disintegrated purposelessness and hopelessness by enclosing all political discourse (Pomerantsev, 2014).

The Kremlin's idea is to own all forms of political discourse, to not let any independent movements develop outside of its walls. Its Moscow can feel like an oligarchy in the morning and a democracy in the afternoon, a monarchy for dinner and a totalitarian state by bedtime.

(Pomerantsev, 2014)

In many ways, Surkov has developed a new rhetoric, one in which identification with a political emptiness and an abiding attitude of skepticism, and a deep mistrust of all movements and discourses, is fostered by constant conflicting spectacles, or what is being called in the West "fake news". His methods fly in the face of almost a century of research, and they seem to be working everywhere, including the United States, in which the body politic is being treated to a federal politics conducted by a four-time-bankrupt billionaire, reality television show host. He has developed a new system of government by Tweet and misdirection. His cabinet is stacked with members of the corporate *comitatus* (Monbiot, 2017).

Note

1 For example, Robert McChesney, Tanner Mirlees, Janet Wasko, Dan Schiller, Doug Kellner, Ian Roderick, Phil Graham, Robin Mansell, Allan and Carmen Luke, Ruth Wodak, and Norman Fairclough.

5 Neofeudal Corporatism and Its Discontents

Almost by definition, feudalism is public power in private hands.
—(Thurow, 1996, pp. 264–265)

This chapter articulates a definition of current circumstances as neofeudal corporatism and connects that definition to the global spread of the CPI's mass rhetorical techniques described in Chapter 4. I define the system as corporatist based on four features: the separation of ownership and control, the subjugation of industry by business, the separation of accountability from responsibility, and the subjugation of going concerns by overriding concerns or crises (Graham and Luke, 2011). I elaborate upon those features below after giving more general defining features of what I mean by neofeudalism and corporatism.

The first thing to note about corporatism is that it is the opposite of what is called "free trade" in which businesses participate in open competition and live or die on their success in "the market". Its central definitive feature is extreme and systematic delegation of government power to the private sector, what is today called "privatisation" of government functions. Whitman (1991) dates American corporatism to Roosevelt's first New Deal. The National Recovery Administration (NRA) was run by General Hugh Johnson and was widely seen as 'a vast scheme for delegating governmental authority to private cartels, . . . akin to the "corporativism" of Italian Fascism', a mode of governance that was publicly favoured in US policy circles until Italy invaded Ethiopia (p. 748). Whitman notes that while corporatism is notoriously difficult to define, all definitions 'involve the delegation of what most lawyers think of as state powers to private organizations' (p. 752).[1] The process of "privatisation" has run rampant since the Reagan–Thatcher years and the rise of what has deceptively been labelled "neoliberalism". The few examples I give below will suffice to show how complex the web of corporatism has become and how thoroughly militarised its character.

But I also think it is essential to establish the system as definitively non-capitalistic for the purposes of appropriate critique.

I use the term neofeudal to point to the thoroughly militaristic and transnational character of the current system. It first refers to the multi-trillion dollar "protection racket" dominated by what Dwight Eisenhower called 'the military industrial complex' (Eisenhower, 1961). Woodrow Wilson announced neofeudal corporatism in 1919 when he said the following to the businessmen of Turin after WWI:

> Perhaps you gentlemen think of the members of your Government and the members of the other governments who are going to confer now at Paris as the real makers of war and of peace. We are not. You are the makers of war and of peace. The pulse of the modern world beats on the farm and in the mine and in the factory. The plans of the modern world are made in the counting house. The men who do the business of the world now shape the destinies of the world, and peace or war is in large measure in the hands of those who conduct the commerce of the world.
>
> (Wilson, 1919)

As with earlier feudalisms, the current age is dominated by the logic of a permanent arms economy in the form of ostensibly nationalised protection rackets (White, 1962). As with previous feudalisms, excess production is diverted to the maintenance of a military class. Most historians of mediaeval feudalism agree that it 'was essentially military, a type of social organization designed to produce and support cavalry' (1962, p. 3). The currently dominant form of social organisation is "designed" to both produce and support high-tech, massive, globally operative military institutions, most of which is owned and operated by transnational corporations and paid for by governments.

Neofeudal corporatism depends on a perpetual state of warfare. Thus, it is characterised not by 'independent enterprise operating in a market-directed economy' as with prevailing descriptions of free market capitalism, but by corporations dependent on

> guaranteed loans and special tax amortization programs to encourage plant expansion in defense-related industries; guarantees of purchase of metals and minerals for stockpile when civilian markets are weak; the near-total reliance of the aircraft-electronics-missiles manufacturers upon government orders for their very existence; and the lobbying by military contractors that results from this reliance.
>
> (Reagan, 1961, p. 569)

It is a political economic formation based on national governments' perceived need for weaponry of increasing sophistication. It consequently depends on a permanent state of perceived threat and enmity because of its reliance on government clientele, and on the need to "sell" imperatives for multi-trillion dollar defence budgets to the public.

There are other similarities between current and mediaeval forms of feudalism, especially in the *comitatus* relationship (Koehl, 1960; Stephenson, 1941, 1943, p. 245). The *comitatus* was the core of the feudal political system and is also the paradigm of today's corporatism. Charlemagne developed the system out of a desire to create a Europe-wide system of political organisation centred in Paris (Stephenson, 1941, p. 793). Land and other tenures were granted to leading members of the *comitatus*, and the system was based on personal loyalties and shared spoils of war. Its features include intense personal loyalties, distribution of tenures and benefices by warlords, claims to a shared transcendental destiny, and the arbitrary and brutal exercise of power. The neofeudal corporate *comitatus* is organised around militaristic and militarising pursuits and is entirely dependent on a rhetoric of crisis for its maintenance. The term committee is derived from *comitatus* and is, in the current era, the basis for the systematic divestment of personal responsibility through the legal mechanisms of corporate "limited liability".

History records that Ida Tarbell's scientific approach to journalism helped to bring about the demise of John Rockefeller's Standard Oil Trust. It also records but rarely notes that, despite Standard Oil having been broken up into 34 smaller corporations, Rockefeller continued to maintain more or less direct control over all its assets and increase his wealth ninefold and became the world's richest man (*The Economist*, 1999). Most of the major corporations that continue to dominate what Eisenhower called 'the military industrial complex' were established during the decades of the late 19th and early 20th centuries and live on, massified, transformed, and global in reach. Its US elements include General Electric, Fox, Westinghouse, Hughes, Ford, Boeing, Lockheed (Martin), IBM, AT&T (Lucent), RCA, Raytheon, General Motors, Universal, General Dynamics, British Aerospace (BAE), Rolls Royce, and Northrop Grumman, among many others. Corporations now blatantly dominate politics across the world, they buy policy and political influence, and determine political and economic directions for vast areas of the world.

Four Defining Features of Corporatism

The Separation of Ownership and Control

By itself, the separation of ownership from control is enough to indicate the passing of capitalism. Almost any systematic definition of capitalism includes reference to private ownership of the means of producing profit. Marxist thinkers have typically assumed an identity between ownership of the means of production and control over those means, over their associated labour processes, and over what gets produced by them. The simplest and most common definition of capitalism is an economic system in which private individuals invest in ownership of assets to increase their wealth through systems of price, profit, competition, and specialised wage labour. Private ownership is so central to definitions of capitalism that the many diverse revolutionary political movements of the last 150 years were unified by the sole aim of achieving social ownership of the means of production, whether by a workers' revolution or state seizure of private assets. Conversely, "free market" advocates from across the political spectrum are unified by their dedication to "privatisation", or transferring state-owned assets into private hands based on the idea that government is inherently inefficient.

As it has turned out, in economically "advanced" countries, social ownership of the means of production has been achieved without any of the benefits hoped for because of how socialisation was achieved. Private corporations have managed to gain control of a public hoard that is collected and centralised through compulsory savings plans called, variously, 401K, superannuation, pension funds, and sovereign wealth funds. It represents the privatisation of national pension systems. That global hoard of compulsory savings is augmented by funds contributed by enthusiastic "mom and pop" investors in the private "floating" of public assets worldwide, such as banks, airlines, urban utilities including water supplies, telecom and power companies, prison systems, and more recently road and transport infrastructure. The total amount invested globally on behalf of all future retirees is almost impossible to calculate, but recent numbers from the OECD (2016) indicate that the United States has a $14.2 trillion hoard of retirement savings, slightly less than it had in 2007 (Bloomberg, 2007), with the total figure worldwide estimated at roughly $25.33 trillion (OECD, 2016).[2]

The result is that, along with the majority of means of production, a large majority of corporate stock, and the abstract instruments of global finance, are now nominally owned by "the workers of the world" through their pension funds, direct shareholdings, and other direct and indirect investment schemes. But because the hoard is overwhelmingly invested at arm's length from the people who have worked to earn it, it is practically impossible for any individual to know exactly what his or her money owns at any given moment, except perhaps in very general terms. And so the largest public corporations are controlled (managed) by people who do not own them on behalf of many millions of people who have no idea what they own. As illustrated by the $6.5 trillion of "securitised mortgage debt" that eventually triggered the 2008 financial crisis, a raft of associated poison practices transforms debt from asset into commodity, allowing it to be consolidated with other debts of a similar class and then resold as a consolidated "pool" of debt. Such practices have become so arcane, so far removed from reality, and so extreme in their separation of ownership from control, that it has become impossible to say how anybody's money relates to ownership in specific terms (Graham, 2006; Graham and Luke, 2011).

Two points are relevant for the present argument. First, the separation of ownership from control has privileged a relatively small managerial *comitatus*, which has emerged as a globally dominant class. It is comprised of corporate board members and an affiliated cadre of investment bankers, insurance brokers, and credit ratings executives who control the combined resources of the world's corporations, large and small, and exercise their power for each other's benefit. Second, the separation of ownership and control is an achievement of rhetoric, from "selling" the idea of "privatisation" in general; to selling compulsory national savings plans to the public (privatising national pension plans); to framing and legislating those plans politically, economically, and financially; to publicly accounting for the gains and losses from those plans to members, shareholders, and other nominal owners; and finally, to selling the idea of transferring control of the hoard over to what is essentially a largely anonymous and private group of corporate managers. For the relatively small corporate *comitatus* that controls the bulk of the global hoard, the pool of "assets" its members control provides a means through which they can exercise power on a hitherto unprecedented scale and scope through the mechanism of a 'controlling interest' (Graham and Luke, 2011).

A "controlling interest" in a corporation can work in surprising ways. In 2003, with just under 15 per cent ownership in NewsCorp, Rupert Murdoch managed to leverage a controlling interest in Hughes Electronics through NewsCorp's stake in Fox, buying the corporation from GM, with the deal being funded by money from GM's pension funds and other funds from the general public. The deal gave Murdoch control of FCC licenses for direct broadcast satellites, a fixed satellite space station, an Earth station, and all terrestrial wireless licenses held by Hughes at the time. The deal was a historic fusion of global corporate interests in military and media. Three global corporate entities—Fox, General Motors, and Hughes gave a single-person control over a global, extra-terrestrial media system. By apparent fiat, the FCC announcement mobilised GM employee benefits in the sale of GM's own asset (Hughes) along with funds from the general public (Graham and Luke, 2011).

GM subsequently went bankrupt in 2009 and, following an initial $13.4 billion government bailout, the company divested itself of pension obligations to 116,000 of its retired workers in a deal with insurer,

Prudential, erasing $26 billion in liabilities from its books by transferring its obligation for a fee of $4.5 billion to the insurer (Muller, 2012). Muller reports the company in 2012 as having a $10 billion shortfall in its future commitments to workers, with an associated plan to divest itself of $71 billion more in commitments over the near term. By 2014, it had become clear that of the $50 billion the US government eventually paid to GM in multiple bailout payments, the government had 'lost $11.2 billion' (Beech, 2014). Beech reports that the US federal government took a 61 per cent stake in GM. By the end of 2015, GM's pension liabilities had been reduced to $95 billion but were now 'underfunded by $21 billion' (Parker, 2016). The trend is clear. The hoard is part of a global corporate raid, perhaps the biggest robbery in history, in which the savings of workers, pensioners, and the public purse of nations are in the process of being "stripped" on behalf of the corporate *comitatus*.

The Subjugation of Industry by Business and Their Subsequent Separation

Veblen (1923) was first to hit upon the idea that the principles of industry and business are in fundamental conflict. Industry is the making and doing of useful things. Business is the buying and selling of things for profit. Veblen made his observation during the early ascendance of corporatism in the early 1920s. Corporatism is in stark contrast to much earlier political economic formations in which craftsmanship was privileged over business, with the doing of business seen to be somewhat "unclean". Knowledge of earlier systems put the corporation in high contrast for Veblen. He showed the corporation was 'a business concern, not an industrial unit'; he could see it was 'a means of making money, not of making goods' (1923, pp. 82–85). The emergence of the corporation was for Veblen the inevitable result of applying the price system to every facet of life to the point at which people 'have come to the conviction that money-values are more real and substantial than any of the material facts in this transitory world' (1923, p. 88).

Only in such a view can health, water, education, environmental sustainability, and the like be understood as "burdens" on the economy. The historical rise of the price system as the primary political reality, in which corporate profits are taken as an index of general economic wellbeing, indicates the infusion of corporate consciousness throughout whole societies. The result is industrial annihilation, as exemplified by the decline of Detroit, Flint, and the many other former industrial centres in the West. Because it slows down the rate of profit, the making of material goods is an impediment to efficiency as measured by business standards. Hence the tendency for corporations to favour trade in abstract financial instruments, casinos, state lotto systems, and any others in which money makes money and nothing else (Graham, 2006).

Seen in the historical context of the subjugation of industry by business, the rationale for the widespread enthusiasm for "corporate expertise" in government, military, health, education, and throughout the public sector becomes one of enthusiasm for cost savings, budget efficiencies, and lower prices: cheaper food, cheaper consumer goods, cheaper health, cheaper education, and cheaper security. If capitalism was the point at which the principles of industry and business were in symbiotic balance, corporatism is marked by an almost complete domination of industry by business. In the financial sector of currency and derivatives trading, business and industry have become completely delinked. The corporatist ideal is a 'friction-free' economy (Gates, 2006) in which buying and selling of money assumes primacy.

Separation of Accountability and Responsibility

The separation of accountability from responsibility is a corollary to separating ownership from control and subjugating industry to business. By accountability I mean a personal duty of care in spending and reporting on financial budgets. By responsibility I mean personal and moral liability for decisions taken about how budgets are formulated and what they are meant to achieve. Industrial subjugation by business has most obviously taken the form of "outsourcing" and "offshoring" industrial processes in a return to the piece work model of industry in the middle ages. An extreme example of how far the outsourcing movement has extended can be seen in the US government's conduct of the numerous wars since the 2003 invasion of Iraq, with contractors comprising the bulk of international forces and support personnel. By 2007, all income taxes paid by workers in the United States earning $100,000 per year or less, or 90 per cent of all personal income taxes collected in the United States, were absorbed by government consultancy bills (Bartlett and Steele, 2007, p. 344). In 2013, under the Obama Administration, legislation aimed at saving $1.1 trillion dollars in government consulting fees was passed into law in the United States. The result was to reduce payments to the 'top 100 federal defense contractors' from an annual cost of $255.6 billion to $238.5 billion (Stott, 2016).

Personal responsibility has been totally diffused by the committee system, and accountability has followed suit. This is nowhere more evident than in the conduct of war. The massive involvement of the corporate sector in US federal defence has not helped its systems of financial control. The US Department of Defense (2017) lists 258 private contracts between January 2016 and January 2017 costing over $255 billion, including nine during January, 2017 totalling more than $1.7 billion, prior to President-elect Trump's inauguration. The state of accounting for defence budgets in the United States, by far the largest discretionary expense for the US government at 53.1 per cent, is magnificently inaccurate. The Inspector General's report for fiscal year 2015 released in August of 2016 found $6.5 trillion unaccounted for (Hesse, 2016). The annual budget for the US military is $600 billion. Scot Paltrow (2013) notes that in 2011, a single office in Columbus, Ohio 'made at least $1.59 trillion . . . in errors' and that all $8.5 trillion paid to the pentagon by the US government between 1996 and 2013 had gone unaccounted for. He reports the frustration of the US Defense Secretary in trying to get the most basic accounting information. Robert Gates, former Secretary of Defense, 'described the Pentagon's business operations as "an amalgam of fiefdoms without centralized mechanisms to allocate resources, track expenditures, and measure results'. He reports not being able to get the most basic information 'such as "How much money did you spend" and "How many people do you have?"' (Paltrow, 2013).

The Pentagon and its accounting branch slate the problem to thousands of different accounting systems being used throughout the defence forces, with one estimate putting the number of different software systems in use at 5,000 (Paltrow, 2013). All that despite the fact that legislation was introduced in 2012 to ensure the Pentagon was "audit ready" by 2017, a clear failure given the $6.5 trillion accounting error of August 2016. The case of the Pentagon accounts is extreme. However, it is emblematic of a trend that defines neofeudal corporatism, which is the systematic avoidance of either moral or financial answerability at a personal level. The Sarbanes-Oxley act of 2002 made little or no difference, as evidenced by the 2008 financial crisis triggered by mortgage derivatives. Frederick Allen notes that ten years after the act, things had not improved, pointing to corporate malfeasance by the *comitatus* as 'the real problem with corporate governance—boards of directors' (Allen, 2012).

Subjugation of Going Concerns by Overriding Concerns

The subjugation of 'going concerns' by overriding concerns refers to the abandonment of sustainable business practices in the face of threatening matters towards which public attention is consciously focused on a mass scale. In such cases, the playing up of some threat is used as a technique of persuasion in what amounts to a series of national or global "emergencies" (Gardner, 2008). The "crisis" is a hallmark of neofeudal corporatism and is unquestionably an achievement of mass rhetoric. The end result is evident in the close links between mass media and military institutions that can be seen almost everywhere throughout the developed world. The United States has a century of developing systematic links between its military and entertainment sectors. GE, Westinghouse, Hughes, Comcast, Disney, Universal, NBC, Fox, NewsCorp, Vivendi, Time Warner, ABC, Thomson Reuters, Associated Press, CBS, and CNN are all entangled in complex ways with military, government, and each other (Mirlees, 2016, pp. 106–109). The trend is the same throughout the developed world; in Europe, Australia, Canada, New Zealand, and elsewhere, media concentration is at an all-time high, with pending mergers between Comcast and Time Warner, and DirecTV and AT&T currently on the books of the FCC (Sallet, 2015).

The idea of a capitalised 'going concern' was the basis upon which 'visible' and 'personal' relationships between owners and workers were first replaced by 'impersonal' management relationships mediated by shareholdings (Veblen, 1923, p. 59). According to Veblen, a '"going concern" . . . was valued and capitalized on its earning capacity; and the businesslike management of industry, accordingly, centred upon the net earnings to be derived in a competitive market' (1923, p. 59). There is a clear and close connection between the demise of the capitalised going concern in favour of a depersonalised model, the functional separation of ownership and control, the institutional subjugation of industry by business, the moral separation of accountability and responsibility, and the practical subjugation of going concerns by overriding concerns, or general states of emergency.

Overriding concerns demand taxes, debts, and levies held against present and future revenues in the interests of public protection against the effects of whatever happens to be the overriding concern (threat) of the day. Because overriding concerns are about something terrifying that could happen in future, mitigation strategies must go beyond certainties of the present to focus public attention on the risks of the future threat. Because they are communicated as public threats on national and international scales, overriding concerns demand a military response—large standing armies, massive weapons industries, police, espionage systems, mass troop deployments, and so on—which is always and necessarily a tax on the future, an ongoing means of ensuring public indebtedness, and the basis of ongoing public indebtedness to private interests.

Overriding concerns are achieved in the contemporary context by the same methods of propaganda worked out by the CPI (Graham and Luke, 2003, 2005, 2011). From Wilson's (1917) war message, in which he stated that 'the world must be made safe for democracy', and that 'the peace of the world and the freedom of its peoples' depended on United States involvement in WWI, to the 1918 US Sedition Act, to the historically influential work of the CPI, Wilson's administration developed the means of producing and maintaining overriding concerns of national and international significance that have persisted ever since. Wilson's war message includes a summary of the future implications for what he was about to do:

> What this will involve is clear. It will involve the utmost practicable cooperation in counsel and action with the governments now at war with Germany, and, as incident to that, the extension to those governments of the most liberal financial credit, in order that our resources may so far as possible be added to theirs. It will involve the organization and mobilization of all the material resources of the country to supply the materials of war and serve the incidental needs of the Nation in the most abundant and yet the most economical and efficient way possible. . . . It will involve also, of course, the granting of adequate credits to the Government, sustained, I hope, so far as they can equitably be sustained by the present generation, by well-conceived taxation.
>
> (Wilson, 1917)

The pattern for the century to come is established: the overriding concern of the day is paid for through 'liberal financial credit' to foreign nations so that they can buy US resources which 'can be added to theirs'; the 'mobilization of all the material resources of the country to supply the materials of war'; and 'the granting of adequate credits' domestically, all of which would hopefully be paid for by tax in the 'present generation', but which ended up being a tax on every generation to follow.

The pragmatic "cash value" of Wilson's speech was the start of a publicly funded bonanza for the businesses that serviced the war machine: bad news for front line soldiers and taxpayers. A system based on overriding concerns necessarily lays claim to future net product as well as present, and therefore requires a general credit (debt) system operating nationally and internationally. The future tense of Wilson's war speech provides a frame for the current political economic system. Debt is money set in future tense and is a claim on future human life. It is therefore perfectly suited to the business aim of ever-increasing money values because the future is a theoretically infinite space that can therefore be infinitely monetised (Graham, 2006).

The Creel century is replete with overriding concerns: two World Wars; the Great Depression; prohibition; the Cold War; Korea; Vietnam; the oil crisis of the 1970s; two Gulf Wars; the Balkans crises; the various and continual wars on drugs, crime, terror, obesity, and poverty; overriding concerns continue through the serial financial crises of peak oil, Savings and Loan, the early 1990s recession, the Asian crisis of the late 1990s, the "dotcom" crash of 2001, and the 2008 Global Financial Crisis; and endless wars of retaliation that have been waged since September 11, 2001, in Iraq, Afghanistan, Yemen, Somalia, and Syria. Highly tuned military and civilian

forces engaged in strategic communication campaigns are utterly necessary to maintain overriding concerns on such a scale for such a sustained
length of time. Economies of massive indebtedness are the inevitable result
of the militarisation that such a state of constant public anxiety entails and
maintains.

The net result of the overriding concern is a political economy based on
fear, a system of communication that continuously streams news of real
and potential terrors. The situation shifts what counts as value in political economic terms and changes the political economic tense system into a
permanent present constantly in fear of its future (Graham, 2006). It moves
everyday choice and agency in the various domains of family, life, and work
towards a moral, economic, and political investment in avoidance, deter-
rence, and a mentality in which action is premised on avoiding imagined
future disaster. It is the basis of the global protection racket that underpins
neofeudal corporatism.

The Future Tense

In business, it is in one's self-interest to increase profits. In war, it is in
one's self-interest to defeat all enemies. Both are future-oriented pursuits.
When we consider the global economic "war of all against all" legislated
for by the Social Darwinism of free marketeers, and situate economic "self-
interest" as being determined within a universal struggle for economic and
military dominance, we see that the system is structured "strategically"
to pit every group against every other and every individual against every
other. What is dressed up as primitive "liberalism", a self-interest functioning unquestionably in the general good, is rather an environment premised
on mutual destruction as a motivation: total and comprehensive war, from
the interpersonal to the international.

Neofeudal corporatism is sustained by threat and debt. Threats and
debts are forms of 'symbolic action' that can work upon whole populations (Burke, 1966). Both move general attention and social perceptions of
value into the future tense, which is also the tense of policy and exhortation in general (Graham, 2006). Both those symbolic mechanisms demand
the backing of military force and concomitant levels of destructive con-
sumption that only begins with armaments. Research, military personnel,
government personnel, public relations campaigns, consulting services,
intelligence services, and many multi-million-dollar movie budgets can all
be put under the banner of military expenditure. When added to security
budgets more generally—police, jails, private security firms, border protection forces, multilateral peacekeeping forces—along with the various and
invariably large bureaucratic, ministerial, and administrative organisations

associated with the combined parts of the military industrial complex, expenditure on organised violence, and its simultaneous suppression, becomes literally incalculable.

Since the 'second age' of feudalism, no political form has achieved such a high degree of distance between ruling elites and the ruled, confusing distinctions between property rights, discretionary control, executive privilege, and military force (cf. Bloch, 1962, pp. 345–354). Like second-age feudalism, our current era is characterised by contractual allegiances underwritten by extreme military force; systematic corporate subjection through ties of indebtedness; 'the rigorous economic subjection' of the great majority of people 'to a few powerful men'; 'the identification of wealth . . . with power'; and the highest of economic priorities being placed on the maintenance of a professional military class (pp. 441–452). Far from being a new source of strength for the nation state, neofeudal corporatism arises from and accelerates a 'profound weakening of the State' (pp. 441–452). At the beginning of 2017, Oxfam reports that the wealthiest eight men in the world 'are worth more than half of the world's population', with a combined personal wealth of $426 billion (Beattie, 2017). In a separate study, 'the Equality Trust found the richest 100 families in Britain have seen their combined wealth increase by at least £55.5billion since 2010' (Beattie, 2017), which is to say since the end of the 2008–2009 global financial crisis. Those numbers are dwarfed by national debt, especially in the United States, which is $19.9 trillion, or roughly 12 times the entire "dollar value" of the world's current wealth as calculated by the Oxfam study and more than a third of all global public debt, which stands at $57.8 trillion (*The Economist*, 2017). Private debt in the United Sates alone stood at over $25 trillion by 2014 (Vague, 2014).

Debt is a means of subjugation. Its mechanisms have been extended globally and infused through every pore of humanity. Constant threats of danger are reiterated and amplified each day, and violence thus becomes an imperative. The perceived experience of violence by victims and perpetrators are formally and technologically indistinguishable from mass entertainments, a fact which became apparent during the attacks on the Pentagon and World Trade Centre of September 11, 2001. Countless people who saw live coverage of the attacks 'thought they were watching a movie' (see, for example, Gray, 2001). Even people personally involved in the devastation said it 'was like watching a movie' (see, for example, Balaghi, 2002). Drone warfare is conducted in the form of a computer game. Between 2011 and April, 2015, there have been an estimated 522 drone strikes in Yemen, Afghanistan, Pakistan, and Somalia killing 3,852 people, including 476 civilians (Shane, 2015). Death at a distance is the norm for organised violence in the West. The summary execution of Osama Bin Laden and subsequent disposal of his body was watched "live" in Washington by the US President and his security staff as it happened (Drury, Williams, and Greenhill, 2011). One account reports the incident as taking the form of a US television show, *24*, which promotes the strategic value of torture and extra-judicial murder based on some emergency:

> The footage of the battle in Bin Laden's Pakistani hideout—which played out like an episode of 24—is said to show one of his wives acting as a human shield to protect him as he blasted away with an AK47 assault rifle. . . . She died, along with three other men, including one of Bin Laden's sons. Within hours, the Al Qaeda leader's body was buried at sea.
>
> (Drury, Williams, and Greenhill, 2011)

The full flower of neofeudal corporatism presents analysis with all kinds of dilemmas and paradoxes. It presents an ironic twist to 'end of nation', 'end of state', 'end of ideology' proclamations of the mid-to-late 1990s when "globalisation" was the slogan. It relies on the most blatant forms of nationalist militarism, including the aggressive promotion of protection at any cost; a powerful expansion of the techniques developed by the CPI; and remote-controlled violence on a global scale. All of this is legitimated by national leaderships, allegedly in defence of national borders, of ways of life that no longer exist, and of non-secular moral orders. At the same time, political leaders make policy for, and on behalf of, transnational corporations who benefit from the conflict, and are themselves at the nexus of corporate and political power.

Nationalism is back, at least in rhetorical form, as exemplified by the incoming reality-television-star-cum-bankrupt, President Trump, who rose to power with his promise to "make America great again". There is no longer talk of "globalisation". The European settlement has begun to break down with Britain voting to leave the EU and others threatening to follow. As the world's most prosperous nations continue towards economic failure, degraded social conditions are leveraged to promote older ways of life, older attitudes and values, and even older structures of governance. In that sense, the emergence of neofeudal corporatism is anachronistic in surprising ways. The rhetoric of neofeudal corporatism is clearly aimed at subordinating merely economic goals to a militaristic nationalism, all the while preying on the lived experience of "commoners" saturated in debt and drenched in projected fear. Like the many militarising movements before it, neofeudal corporatism disguises its vested interests in the tattered drag of "national interest", and, however quietly put, in the hierarchical reordering and revaluation of persons along crude lines of race, "creed", morality, and other perennial rhetorics of Othering.

Notes

1 In all discussions by extreme conservatives, such as Grover Norquist who wants 'to shrink government to the size where we can drown it in a bathtub', the one thing they see as being a public good, and therefore the sole legitimate province of government, is 'a strong military' (Farmer, 2008, p. 73). That is in fact the core feature that drives neofeudal corporatism and its multi-trillion-dollar annual defence budgets and is at the centre of "big" government.
2 It is worth noting that the figure was also just over $25 trillion in 2007 (Appell, 2007), indicating that even the financial system of hypercapitalism has stalled (Graham, 2006).

6 The Military Entertainment Complex

Then and Now

This chapter links the "military entertainment complex" of the CPI era with that of today, showing the underlying techniques that join both eras. There is an unbroken history of cooperation in the United States among the institutions of war and those of entertainment that begins with the Committee on Public Information (CPI) (Mirlees, 2016; Graham and Luke, 2003). The upshot of the institutional marriage in the United States is the extent and cost of contemporary militarisation. Today we cannot separate militarisation along public–private lines, between individual and collective interests, or between general cultural activity and specifically military activity. Among the largest corporate manufacturers of military hardware can be found some of the world's largest finance companies (General Electric, General Motors); telecommunications companies (Siemens, Texas Instruments); media organisations (CBS, NBC); manufacturers of aeroplanes (Boeing, McDonnell Douglas); household appliances (Samsung, General Electric); and cars (General Motors, Rolls Royce, Mitsubishi, Fiat, Daimler-Benz). Even the term "blockbuster", denoting the success of a film, is derived from the name of a bomb designed to level large sections of cities during WWII.

The US Department of Defense (DoD) takes an explicitly militarised view of narrative in achieving its outcomes (Miskimmon, O'Loughlin, and Roselle, 2014). Narrative is a part of military strategy, and 'the battle of the narrative' is 'a full-blown battle in the cognitive dimension of the information environment' (DoD, 2010, p. xiii). Militaristic use of narrative is as old as recorded civilization. Pedagogic use of militaristic narrative is just as old (Havelock, 1963). The difference today is the speed, mass, and immersive realism of the kinds of narrative experiences involved in the "soft power" of nations. From massive 3D IMAX cinemas to 3D, first-person shooter games, to intense interpersonal social media battles that are so emotionally consuming as to lead to suicide and murder, today's audience member has the means for total involvement in a communication environment dominated by ongoing crises, threats, risks, and enmities.

As Arnold Pacey (1999/2001) points out, extreme and explicit violence being staple themes in mass entertainment are of concern because the relationships that emerge between entertainmentised representations of violence, military-mindedness, strategic communication, and actual mass murder become more rather than less obviously direct the more closely the relationships are investigated. Those relationships are at the centre of neofeudal corporatism. Thomas Friedman puts them like this:

> The hidden hand of the market will never work without a hidden fist—McDonald's cannot flourish without McDonnel Douglas . . . the hidden fist that keeps the world safe for Silicon Valley's technologies is called the United States Army, Air Force, Navy and Marine Corps.
>
> (1999, p. 84)

Peak Entertainment

As I write, the United States is inaugurating a new president who left his position as a reality television show host to take to the presidential campaign trail. He has walked directly into the White House from a television show in which he became famous for the phase, "You're fired!" *The Apprentice* is themed as entertainment based on a combination of raw ambition and public humiliation as the main ingredients of a competition, the winning prize for which is a brief tenure at the lowest levels of the corporate *comitatus*. President Trump has been replaced on the show by ex-bodybuilder, action movie star, and former Governor of California, Arnold Schwarzenegger. After Schwarzenegger's first appearance on the show, the president-elect insulted the new host with a Twitter tirade for having low ratings, blaming the fall on Schwarzenegger's support for presidential rival, Hillary Clinton.

The current scenario is a more bizarre and extreme extension of trends that began to take shape with the election of Ronald Reagan to the US Presidency in 1981. Reagan, a former B-Grade actor, sports radio announcer, anti-communist union organiser, and California Governor, laid the legislative groundwork for the mass selloff of US public assets to banking interests that began in the 1980s and continues today. Hulk Hogan, Jesse Ventura, Clint Eastwood, Paul Grandy (Gopher from *The Love Boat*), Sonny Bono, and Fred Thompson are just a few of the more high-profile celebrities who have moved into US politics since. The politics of celebrity work in multiple ways in the new environment. The question of who was and who was not going to perform at the Trump inauguration took up much ink and oxygen, with even a Springsteen tribute band, the B Street Boys, withdrawing from the event and attracting global publicity in the process.

Jason Newman (2017) of *Rolling Stone* reports on the E Street band members' Twitter feeds in response to the B Street band's involvement in the inaugural event:

> Garry Tallent, the E Street Band's founding bassist, tweeted, in response to news of the B-Street band's appearance, "Please tell me this is more fake news. Or at least a joke." Steven Van Zandt, the group's outspoken guitarist, tweeted of the B-Street Band, "Nice guys. Met them. I wouldn't say right or wrong. Up to them. But it's naive to think one can separate Art and Politics. Art IS Politics."
>
> (Newman, 2017)

There has been much written about the notion of entertainmentisation of politics both before and since Neil Postman's (1985) *Amusing Ourselves to Death*. The trend has turned back on itself, and now we are seeing the increasing politicisation of entertainment and entertainers. Some pundits have begun to call it "The Kardashian Effect", a public obsession with the opinions, habits, and daily carrying on of celebrities.

Hence entertainers have begun to play increasingly significant roles in politics, and entertainment has been politicised to an unprecedented degree. The Obama inauguration in 2009 was a public event involving A-List entertainers whose performances functioned as a public political endorsement:

> Obama's inauguration celebrations will feature some of the world's most famous celebrities. On Sunday afternoon alone, the lineup will be dazzling. Among those who have agreed to sing at the opening inaugural event at the Lincoln Memorial are Bruce Springsteen, Bono, Beyoncé Knowles, Stevie Wonder, Shakira, Garth Brooks, Mary J. Blige, Sheryl Crow, Renee Fleming, John Legend, and Usher. In addition, historical passages will be read by Jamie Foxx, Queen Latifah, and Denzel Washington (along with Martin Luther King III).
>
> "We will have the statue of Abraham Lincoln looking down on our stage and a crowd of hundreds of thousands of people lining the mall— a tableau any director would relish," says Don Mischer, who is helping to arrange the festivities. Mischer is perhaps best known for producing the opening ceremonies at the 2002 Winter Olympics and halftime shows at Super Bowls.
>
> (Walsh, 2009)

The idea of a presidential inauguration as a mass "tableau" for rapturous spectacle is pure Goebbels in terms of technique. The symbolism of Lincoln looking down upon a crowd of hundreds of thousands as they participate in a combined pop concert and national literary event, with readings delivered by global superstars is utterly compelling, a "pure" rhetoric of identification aimed at symbolising youth, nationalism, provenance, destiny, progress, celebrity, and high glamour—in total, *Success*, the American dream circa 2009.

The Trump event was always going to be something different. For celebrities and large numbers of elected Democrats, public refusal to attend the inauguration became a political badge of honour. So as far as entertainers went, Trump was left with a 16-year-old former reality television opera star, the Mormon Tabernacle Choir, some pop stars from the turn of the century, and a lineup of lesser country stars (ABC, 2017). While the bill for entertainment was no doubt much cheaper than Obama's 2009 event, Trump's inauguration set an all-time record for political donations. After having threatened to cancel Lockheed-Martin's contract to deliver the $1.5 trillion F-35 fighter plane, which has had massive cost overruns and an endless series of technical problems (Bender, 2015), Trump publicly reported having asked the CEO of Boeing to pitch against it with a version of their F-18 Hornet. As with most of Trump's policies so far, he announced the threat to McDonnell Douglas using Twitter. He posted the announcement the day after meeting with 'chief executives of both aerospace companies, using the bully pulpit to press them on projects he says are too expensive' (Reuters, 2016). Boeing sponsored Trump's inauguration for a million dollars, with international gambling moguls Sheldon and Miriam Adelson allegedly sponsoring the event for even more (Fandos, 2015). All told, the inauguration was set to raise $100 million in donations, almost doubling the previous record of $53 million set by Obama in 2009 (Fandos, 2015).

The event has public and private aspects, with the lack of show business personalities being almost irrelevant to the main purpose of inauguration which is fundraising and private access to the presidency. Fandos (2015) puts it this way:

> Mr. Trump's most prolific donors will gain access to what amounts to a parallel inauguration week, carefully planned and largely out of public sight, during which they can mingle with members of the incoming administration over intimate meals and witness Mr. Trump's ascension from the front rows. . . . ethics experts say Mr. Trump's donors are being given greater access and facing fewer limits on donations than those in other recent inaugurations, despite his vow to "drain the swamp" of special interests in Washington.
>
> (Fandos, 2015)

The analytical point here is not that there is anything particularly unusual about Trump using his inauguration as a fundraiser, nor even that he has set a record. It is that the news of his fundraising success; the degree to which corporates are being granted personal access to political decision makers during the event; and the fact that such a lucrative, indulgent, and overtly corporatist approach goes against the basic principles of the Trump campaign, have been obscured by a flood of trivial news about progressive-minded celebrities and Democrat politicians refusing to attend the event, about groups planning to protest his presidency, and about who is performing at the event.[1]

Journalism in the early 21st century is the full realisation of Postman's thesis on entertainmentisation. With its Latin root *tenere* meaning "to hold", the word "entertainment" goes directly to public attention. Following Lippmann's (1922) observation that nobody could possibly have the time or energy to pay attention to everything given a world newly connected and massified by communication technologies, Harold Lasswell (1941) first drew theoretical attention to the importance of attention itself, with Davenport and Beck (2001) later "economising" the concept once the internet had begun to further complicate outcomes of mediated rhetoric. Had the many pundits predicting Trump's failure, first at winning the Republican candidacy and then the Presidency, read Lasswell or understood how heavily the attention of the public mind is pressed upon in the current environment, they would have revised either their predictions or their habit of amplifying each outrageous tweet Trump issued during the campaign. The age-old dictum, often attributed to P. T. Barnum, that "any publicity is good publicity" continues to hold true. A simple count of Trump's media mentions in comparison to those of his primary and presidential rivals demonstrates the overwhelming amount of attention he garnered with his methods, regardless of whether it was positive or negative (Leetaru, 2017a). In 2015–2016, Trump received 1,398,873 mentions on national television news compared to Hillary Clinton's 649,886 (Leetaru, 2017a). He consistently topped web news by percentage of total mentions (Leetaru, 2017b). His trolling strategy on Twitter proved successful in the Republican primaries, gaining him 46 per cent of Google News mentions, more than 300 per cent more than his closest rival, Jeb Bush, with similar percentage differences for television news (Leetaru, 2015).

Of course, to assert that mere mentions determined the election would be overly simplistic and quite probably incorrect, but as an indicator, it seems to be fairly reliable. The evidence for attention is compelling. We see a clear correlation between relative number of mentions on social media for Trump and Clinton and the relative number of mentions on television and newspapers, though seemingly none of the polling pundits made the connection or thought about the figures with the basics of 'audience labour' in mind (Smythe, 1981):

> The underlying principle is simple: Where the attention goes, the money will inevitably follow. And right now, the attention of a large chunk of the population is being diverted away from traditional content

and information channels, and platforms like Facebook and Google are busy vacuuming it up.

(Ingram, 2015)

Ingram is making a statement here about what is essentially an advertising model, what Dallas Smythe (1981) called 'audience labour', and which has also been called "the battle for attention", "the battle for eyeballs", and so on. But the implications of attention do not stop at the corporate advertising dollar. Politics operates on exactly the same principles, as does corporate public diplomacy (Chadwick, 2014). They must also follow the "eyeballs".

The striking social media statistics collected by *Tech Crunch* show that as the total number of engagements with the social media activities of each candidate rose, positive sentiment fell for both (Perez, 2016). A leaked video that showed an outrageous degree of misogyny on the part of Trump actually helped his campaign:

> It seems . . . that Trump benefitted from that old adage, "any press is good press." . . . While the October 7th leak of the Access Hollywood tape was reported as a low moment in the Trump campaign, it expanded his social media audience more than any other until Election Day.
>
> (Perez, 2016)

That is the tape in which Trump said of women that, 'when you're a star, they let you do it, . . . You can do anything . . . Grab them by the pussy . . . You can do anything' (cited in Fahrenthold, 2016). The same happened during his Iowa campaign in which he claimed that he 'could stand in the middle of 5th Avenue and shoot somebody' and not lose any votes (in Diamond, 2016). The possible implications of his strategy being successful are strange and disturbing. One possibility is that Trump won the election simply because he was the most entertaining candidate (while realising that Clinton won the popular vote). Another is that politics has entered the realm of pantomime, with trolling becoming a new form of scapegoating, a kind of symbolic killing through which audiences achieve catharsis, identification with particular morés, and an associated "cleansing" achieved through the annihilation of sacrificial symbols (Burke, 1950/1969). Another possibility is that the strenuous tedium of endless political messages promoting simultaneous and contradictory values of freedom, security, terror, democracy, competition, globalism, nationalism, austerity, economic and military adventurism, hope, hopelessness, individualism, and unity has created the conditions in which simplistic messages featuring "common sense" ways to "fix" things with the political equivalent of a "punch in the face" appear attractive to large numbers of voters. That last is often summed up as people being tired of "politics as usual" along with losing their means of living, while the "one percent" gets stinking rich. Another possibility is that the valorisation of business has finally reached the point at which the only viable presidential candidate is one with CEO experience, as gambling mogul Adelson claimed of Trump, a side effect of neofeudal corporatism's unrelenting emphasis on the importance of business values and practices in every aspect of life.

Whatever the reasons for Trump's win, they are no doubt complex and various. What is clear, though, is that Trump's presidency is a direct and total integration of the military industrial complex with global entertainment industries. The United States has elected an Entertainer-In-Chief who communicates policy and opinion by what have been termed 'tweedicts' (Reich, 2017). The Press Secretary for Trump's government, Sean Spicer, says that Trump's tweets 'direct the news cycle' (Hensch, 2017). Robert Reich, Secretary of Labor under Clinton, argues that in 'driving the news'

> Trump's tweedicts gain the power of implied threats—that he'll, for example, sanction a particular company (Ford, General Motors, Carrier or Boeing); unilaterally alter foreign policy (recognize Taiwan, encourage Israel to expand on the West Bank, not back NATO against Russian aggression); unleash his angry followers on a particular critic (a local union leader in Michigan, a teenage girl in New Hampshire, a TV news host); cause customers or readers to boycott a media outlet (CNN, the Arizona Republican, "Saturday Night Live," the cast of "Hamilton"); or impose high political costs on Republican members of Congress (for pursuing an investigation against Russia, gutting an ethics office).
>
> (Reich, 2017)

Trump communicates local, national, and global policy in messages of 140 characters or less, sent to the world at large, and amplified by the popular press, doing so even prior to his inauguration. It is the ultimate in aggressive, individualistic, competitive, strategic communication.

Following his election, events that looked to be straight from the pages of *The Manchurian Candidate* began to unfold around Trump's relationship with Russian President Putin. A security dossier, also known as "Pee-Gate", allegedly written by former British spy and Director of Orbis security, Christopher Steele, was anonymously leaked to the global press (Sengupta, 2017). Trump responded with a series of tweets denouncing the dossier as a 'false and fictitious report that was illegally circulated' and Steele as a 'failed spy' (Sengupta, 2017). The dossier and its media commentary were followed by another Twitter outburst by Trump, aimed at the Central Intelligence Agency (CIA), National Security Agency (NSA), Federal Bureau of Investigation (FBI), and the Director of National Intelligence, blaming US intelligence agencies for leaking the dossier and equating the intelligence community with 'Nazi Germany' (Guardian, 2017). Trump's public bashing of US intelligence appears even stranger when considering the unprecedented mid-election letter from FBI Director James Comey announcing that Hillary Clinton was again under investigation for using a personal email server during her tenure as Secretary of State, an event which some pundits claim cost Clinton the election (Osborne, 2016).

At the time of writing, issues of Russian espionage and its influence on the presidential election, along with Trump's response to the US intelligence agencies, continue to wane in their ability to command the news cycle as the press continues its reports on the guest list for the inauguration, produces a string of unflattering stories about the new US Cabinet nominees, and details their ignorant or unethical performances at Congressional confirmation hearings (Tumulty, Wagner, and O'Keefe, 2017). The Gallup polls had Trump at an historically low approval rating for a president leading up to inauguration. Trump responded to those polls with a tweet indicating he was unimpressed with the numbers, saying the 'same people who did the phony election polls, and were so wrong, are now doing approval rating polls. They are rigged just like before' (Baker, 2017). The present theme runs in direct opposition to that of a century ago which was characterised by pragmatic science and its aim of government by science and fact. The current theme is marked by terms like 'fake news', 'post-truth era', and 'post-fact world' (see, for example, Coughlan, 2017).

The CPI's role in censorship, with which Lippmann (1922) was so concerned, is either impossible or irrelevant in current circumstances: impossible because any information can be spread globally in an instant; irrelevant because there is so much information in so many forms, from so many sources, being disseminated at such a rate that the likelihood of anything being memorable apart from the most massive media spectacles that Postman's "Now . . . this" of the television era has sped up and intensified so as to achieve a permanent amnesia in the public mind (Postman, 1985, Ch. 7).

> "Now . . . this" is commonly used on radio and television newscasts to indicate that what one has just heard or seen has no relevance to what one is about to hear or see, or possibly to anything one is ever likely to hear or see. The phrase is a means of acknowledging the fact that the world as mapped by the speeded-up electronic media has no order or meaning and is not to be taken seriously. There is no murder so brutal, no earthquake so devastating, no political blunder so costly—for that matter, no ball score so tantalizing or weather report so threatening—that it cannot be erased from our minds by a newscaster saying, "Now . . . this."
>
> (1985, p. 99)

In any case, links between facts, truth, accurate reporting of the world, general understandings of the world, and moral outcomes (besides the value of truthfulness itself) are tenuous at best: the more discussion about factuality, the less discussion about what is good and why. Scientism has swamped dramatism for most of the last century, bringing with it spectacular technological results, unbridled partisanship at every level, and social and economic inequality on a global scale unrivalled since that of Europe in the days leading up to WWI (Picketty, 2014, p. 248–249). Today the focus is on true/false binaries of populist scientism, as exemplified by such websites as *I Fucking Love Science* (IFLS, 2017a), which has recently teamed up with *The Science Channel* to dispel internet 'quacks' and 'curate the best science content on the web' (2017a). The terms and conditions for using the IFLS site warrant nothing of the sort: 'The service, including all content therein, is provided "as is" and without warranties of any kind either express or implied and you shall use the service at your own risk' (IFLS, 2017b). The site is funded by advertising and so features attention grabbing stories and sub-heads like 'Blonde-Haired Moth With Small Genitals Named After Donald Trump' (IFLS, 2017c). IFLS has a Facebook audience of 25 million and, despite being fact based and undoubtedly focused on genuine science, is pure entertainment.

The truth or otherwise of news stories seems to have had very little to do with Trump's election in any case. A survey of 1,208 US adults in late November, 2016, using a mixture of true, false, and placebo headlines indicate that, to have an effect on the election, 'a single fake news story would need the persuasive power of 36 TV campaign ads' (Allcott and Gentzkow, 2017; Robertson, 2017). The study also notes that for 57 per cent of respondents, television is their main and most trusted source for news. The authors of the study concluded that, 'using the difference between actual and placebo stories as a measure of true recall' 1.2 per cent of people remember an 'average' news story (Allcott and Gentzkow, 2017, p. 3). The study shows again that, based on 'Facebook shares', stories about Trump were shared four times as often as those about Clinton (p. 3).

And all of the described above is interesting if you believe statistics. Davies (2017) argues convincingly that the statistical era is over because the state itself has become a meaningless distinction in the face of global data regimes. Statistics have their origin in Francis Bacon's idea for an expert class of Statists and were originally called statics (Ranney, 1976). The concept of statistics was historically tied to the modern state. Today, there is a new development in the collection of numbers about people, their opinions, and the direction of society, and data 'accumulates by default' through social media and 'sweeping digitisation' in general. The more our 'cities, cars, homes and household objects become digitally connected, the amount of data we leave in our trail will grow even greater. In this new world, data are captured first and research questions come later' (Davies, 2017).

All of which points to the probability that "big data" will become a merely forensic affair. Davies argues that the new social categories are ones of identification, 'a way of tracking the identities that people bestow upon themselves (such as "#ImwithCorbyn" or "entrepreneur") rather than imposing classifications upon them' prior to analysis (Davies, 2017). In enumerating the problems of big data, Davies points to a lack of scalar boundaries because of the global character of the internet, the fact that most people are 'totally oblivious' about what our data "say" about us, and that 'there is nothing that anchors this new capacity in the public interest or public debate'. His concern is that commercially generated and owned data are potentially of use to populists after their analysis by 'a new, less visible elite, who seek out patterns from vast data banks, but rarely make any public pronouncements', and who are trained in either mathematics or physics rather than any social science disciplines. He fears a 'post-statistical society is a potentially frightening proposition' because it 'drastically privatises' knowledge about public opinion and removes 'one of the many pillars of liberalism'. But what Davies seems to miss is that knowledge about public opinion has been privatised for close to a century, along with its means of manipulation. Also, he seems to forget the saying attributed to (among many others) Arthur Balfour (Lee, 2016): 'There are three kinds of lies: lies, damned lies, and statistics'. That is simply to say that many statistics which are technically perfect in mathematical terms can be either meaningless, irrelevant, qualitatively damaged by the semantics of their design, or distort outcomes through the kinds of narrowly focused motivations that they institute, such as in areas of university performance indicators or school testing regimes (Scott, 2016).

In case my foray into critique of statistical method seems off topic, it is essential to note that "statistics" are the basis of the largest entertainment sector on the globe: gambling, which was worth \$423 billion in 2014 alone (Cohen, 2015), over two-thirds the size of the US military budget for that year. As at today, I can bet on the outcome of the 2020 US presidential election. Trump has the inside running as incumbent at 2.75 to 1 with Jill Stein and Gary Johnson trailing the field on Australia markets with their odds at 201-to-1. Dwayne "The Rock" Johnson, George Clooney, and Chelsea Clinton are all at 101-to-1 (Sportsbet, 2017). Kim Kardashian is at 275-to-1 on Paddypower (Paddypower, 2017). Such is the degree to which all aspects of public life have become entertainmentised and marketised that the results of elections can often be predicted more reliably by gambling odds—or 'prediction markets' as gambling is now being called by theorists—than they are by statistical polling methods (Erikson and Wlezien, 2012; Levingstone, 2016).

Then and Now: Genre, Media, and Institutional Parasitism

The thread of entertainmentisation that runs from the CPI's nationalising and war-mongering efforts through to the almost entirely unpredictable patterns of civic disintegration evident throughout societies everywhere today can be summed up as a form of textual parasitism, specifically genre parasitism, in which those wishing to partake in the power of a specific institution must first take up that institution's genres, whether text types or action types. To give an example that makes the concept clear, the sermon form in mediaeval Europe became a contested genre when the Aragonese kings began claiming the right to deliver sermons to the public (Graham, 2001; Cawsey, 1999). In contesting the generic form belonging to the institution of the Church, the kings were claiming what was later to be called 'divine right' (Graham, 2001). That is to say, being the primary institution for the value of Divinity, the Church jealously protected its genres because, for any institution, its genres are the recognisable forms through which it interacts with the world. Genres can be text types, like a newspaper article, or activity types, like a graduation ceremony or a State of the Union address (Lemke, 1995, pp. 31–32). Form has a rhetoric of its own (Burke, 1950/1969, 1931/1968). Genres are established forms tied to the values represented by specific institutions, and they function to both 'elicit and solicit expectations' (Graham, 2001, 2002). As an institution purporting to be the organ of important truths and democratic values, news was a natural target for the CPI. Using the institution of news as means of propagating the values of business was already common practice by the time the CPI began.

The practice of placing sponsored news stories in newspapers—originally called "press agentry", and which formed the bulk of early public relations work—relied heavily on a rhetoric of form, of making certain that what was presented to newspaper editors looked and "felt" like news. By the time Ivy Lee wrote his 'declaration of principles' for publicity, press agentry had already gotten a reputation for deceptiveness. Hence Lee's defensive framing of his new venture:

> This is not a secret press bureau. All our work is done in the open. We aim to supply news. This is not an advertising agency; if you think any of our matter ought properly to go to your business office, do not use it. Our matter is accurate. Further details on any subject treated will be supplied promptly, and any editor will be assisted most cheerfully in verifying directly any statement of fact. Upon inquiry, full information will be given to any editor concerning those on whose behalf an article is sent out.

> (Lee, 1905, in Russell and Bishop, 2005)

The strange history of "publicity" as a technical term begins with Henry Adams (1902) whose idea was that publicity should underpin the move to protect the public against the secrecy of the trusts. His motivation was that businesses had grown so large and powerful that he believed it no longer feasible to keep their goings on secret, that the public and government simply had to have a system for what is now called "transparency". Jonathan Auerbach (2015) shows that Dewey had been agitating along very similar lines, both in terms of the need for public transparency in all matters bearing upon the body politic, and in seeing 'publicity' as we see the term transparency (p. 98). The same definition of publicity holds for Lippmann up to and beyond *Public Opinion* (Jansen, 2012). The earliest publicity agents, later to be called public relations professionals, were typically journalists (Russell and Bishop, 2005). Ivy Lee was a former business reporter for the *New York Times*. Bernays also began his professional life a journalist. Carl Byoir was a distribution manager for Randolph Hearst's magazines. Each of them realised the rhetorical value of news genres in an age during which scientific facts commanded both the public imagination and in which the prevailing theory of democracy included the idea that truth and democracy were totally linked concepts (see, for example, Barry, 2016). They learned from the CPI which took genre parasitism to new levels. It succeeded by centralising the appropriation of text-type and action genres that were ready to hand and formed active parts of the social fabric: newspapers, magazines, any regular public gatherings, movies, visual art, outdoor spaces, every kind of community association and gathering, religious groups, photography, popular song, and any other generic form it could draw into its organisation.

After the war came the public recriminations. With the widening realisation that the United States had been drawn into a war that people did not really understand, to end in a peace that did not satisfy the collective vitriol of the country's manufactured "war will", and after finding out the extent to which propaganda and censorship had shaped public understandings of the war effort, the US public became outraged (Brown, 2003). Anti-propaganda campaigns have continued in the United States through to the present day (Cone, 2005). Most of those efforts have focused on truth, lies, censorship, or all three. It could be said that, based on a scientism that has only increased in intensity over the last century, studies of public opinion have been increasingly hostile to the notion of opinion itself, which is and always has been the realm of rhetoric rather than science. But a scientistic view cannot attempt analysis of generic parasitism and other issues that are central to the operation of propaganda and the offence it causes simply because they are not susceptible to evaluation in terms of truth.

From the point of view of a dramatistic analysis of form, there is nothing so honest as advertising—except for what it says and how it says it. The point is that, by definition, advertising does not pretend to be anything else other than a commercially motivated message aimed at moving an audience to some sort of action or attitude. Marshall McLuhan (1964) notes the paradoxical attraction of advertising forms:

> During the Second War, the U.S.O. sent special issues of the principal American magazines to the Armed Forces, with the ads omitted. The men insisted on having the ads back again. Naturally. The ads are by far the best part of any magazine or newspaper. More pains and thought, more wit and art go into the making of an ad than into any prose feature of press or magazine. Ads are news. What is wrong with them is that they are always *good* news.
>
> (McLuhan, 1964)

McLuhan thus described advertising as 'the greatest art form of the 20th Century' and was inducted into the Canadian Marketing Hall of Legends in 2015 for his efforts in helping people understand that. I take this brief detour into McLuhan's unusual take on advertising to advance the idea that truth has almost nothing to do with the kinds of offence and outrage typically caused by the practice of strategic communication and its central methods of generic parasitism. Such offence, I argue, has more to do with what Burke calls "piety" (1935/1984, p. 74); the role of piety in reaction to the corruption of sacred symbols through surreptitious parasitism; and the associated hijack of institutional values to arouse antipathy, crisis, fervour, or whatever attitude it might be, either for or against a specific group, idea, service, or product.

Efforts to teach 'critical literacy' through advertising are long and legion (see, e.g., Papadopoulou and Babalioutas, 2007 for an example and review of the literature). Yet, even where, say, issues of gender representation in advertising are concerned, an understanding of pietistic concerns are essential in order to not miss or mistake the critical point. From the perspective of pragmatic moral theory, habits are key to understanding the social and cultural offence caused by parasitism. Habits are 'shaped by prior experience' and begin 'in the instruction (either formal or by example) we received growing up' (Lafollette, 2000, p. 403). Moral habits are no different than any other habit. They are taught and learned, emphasised, de-emphasised, or discarded (p. 406). Since any act 'can affect others' interests', all action has a moral dimension and the 'aim of moral education is to make us habitually sensitive to the needs of others, and to shape the ways we think about, consider, and promote their interests' (p. 407). From such a perspective, then, morals are socialised *patterns of judgement* and are therefore often sacred in magnitude for those who are socialised into them. Burke frames this as a form of secular piety, noting that 'piety is not confined to the strictly religious sphere' and is more about 'loyalty to the sources of our being' and the 'first patterns of judgement' we learn as children (Burke, 1935/1984, p. 71). 'Piety is *the sense of what properly goes with what*' in a given social or cultural context (p. 74). The pieties of the altar can be compared with those of the street gang or the advertising agency, noting that one can be "pious" in terms of any or all of those institutions. A given form of piety is 'a schema of orientation, since it involves the putting together of experiences' (p. 76). And that is the critical aspect of genre parasitism that has gone largely unrecognised, even in the literature concerned with mass rhetoric.

Former Nixon speech writer (and minor cult figure from *Ferris Bueller's Day Off*), Ben Stein, has something to teach us about the kinds of genre parasitism currently causing ructions on a worldwide, geopolitical scale. He is a recently converted Trump supporter who remains bitter about the treatment Nixon received from the press. Following W. Mark Felt's revelation that he was the Watergate whistleblower who informed on the Nixon Presidency for its crimes, Stein accused him, Woodward, and Bernstein of 'smug arrogance and contempt' 'on the grounds that their exposé "hatched the worst nightmare imaginable: genocide," . . . a reference to the Khmer Rouge in Cambodia, who rose to power partially as a result of America's withdrawal from Vietnam' (McGeough, 2017). He seems happy that the press has been put in its place by Trump.

> They're not running the show any longer. One tweet from Trump blows their 5000-word stories to bits. This battle over Trump's legitimacy is done. In Trump's mind and in his legions' minds, he's legitimate and the media isn't. He knows how the world works. It really is a reality TV show.
> (Stein, 2017, in McGeough, 2017)

Nothing I have said here is to suggest that advertising has not played upon the very worst and most destructive pieties and impulses to make its point over the years. It is rather to suggest that advertising has been the most generically "honest" form as compared to, say, public relations, public diplomacy, psychological operations, or even the more overt and blatant types of parasitism, such as product placement in television and movies or "branding" in sports sponsorship.

There are apparently new heights to be reached though. Today, as I write, President Trump has been sworn in, and the White House website quickly featured a section touting 'Melania Trump's modelling and jewellery line' (Snell, 2017). Issues of piety quickly intervened upon the very latest in generic parasitism.

Early on Friday, the website listed the brand names of Trump's jewelry lines sold on QVC. But the website was updated after the publication of this story to remove any mention of QVC.

The original passage read: "Melania is also a successful entrepreneur. In April 2010, Melania Trump launched her own jewelry collection, 'Melania™ Timepieces & Jewelry,' on QVC," the site read.

The updated version of the site now says: "Melania is also a successful entrepreneur. In April 2010, Melania Trump launched her own jewelry collection."

(Snell, 2017)

That is an excellent example of why generic parasitism enrages people. There is not a single issue of truth involved in the example above. It is entirely a matter of piety, or appropriateness. The First Lady having her jewellery line advertised on the White House website is reminiscent of a scene from *Idiocracy*, if its fictional president, Dwayne Elizondo Mountain Dew Herbert Camacho ('porn superstar and five-time ultimate smackdown wrestling champion') had been married (see multimedia links section). Given its success to date, the Trump regime is likely to continue with the same strategic approach to genre parasitism, regardless of whether the new president eventually has to hand over his cell phone for a new secure account with the @POTUS Twitter account to carry his daily tweedicts instead of the @ realDonaldTrump account. That is clear from Trump's choice of cabinet nominees.

Take, for example, Andrew Pudzer, burger magnate and Trump nominee for US Labor Secretary. His restaurants have the highest reported sexual assault rates in the United States, with 56 per cent of 564 female employees reporting having been sexually abused by patrons. Pudzer is proud of the effect he has had on the businesses he runs.

The man at the top of this particular food chain has repeatedly made sexist statements and expressed his backing for the infamous adverts that have objectified and sexualised women's bodies to sell hamburgers for CKE restaurants chains including Carl's Jr. "We believe in putting hot models in our commercials, because ugly ones don't sell burgers," Puzder said, in a 2009 press release. Last year he proudly endorsed the adverts, and stated: "I like beautiful women eating burgers in bikinis . . . I used to hear that brands take on the personality of the CEO. And I rarely thought that was true, but I think this one, in this case, it kind of did take on my personality."

(Bates, 2017)

Only two of Trump's nominees had been approved by the time of his inauguration: Secretary of Defense, General James "Mad Dog" Mattis, and Secretary of Homeland Security, General John Kelly. Both are retired generals, with Trump, as one of his first acts as president, having to sign a waiver for Mattis because the law requires that the head of defence 'must be a civilian and the general had not been retired from the military for at least seven years' (Caldwell, 2017). Mad Dog is 'devoted to gaining full value from every taxpayer dollar spent on defence, thereby earning the trust of Congress and the American people' (in Caldwell, 2017). Perhaps he has not seen the latest Pentagon accounts.

What's Not Here

There is much more to be said on the degree to which the military entertainment complex has permeated society, and how communication industries shape culture. I refer the reader to the work of Tanner Mirlees, Janet Wasko, Noam Chomsky, James Der Derian, Dan Schiller, Robert McChesney, Vincent Mosco, and Ian Roderick for excellent and detailed histories on various other aspects of the problem.

Note

1 A restricted Google News search of terms "Donald Trump" and "Inauguration" on January 18, 2017, returned 80 million results. In the first hundred results, the news topics listed are restricted to those I have mentioned here except for one identifying the fact that he is considering (again announced by Twitter) removing the pressroom from the White House, one about the inauguration lunch menu, two apparently apocryphal stories about Trump having commissioned a poem denigrating his presidential predecessor, and five about a scalper who says he is losing money trying to sell tickets to the event.

7   As We Disappear . . .

This book began with a plan. I had been thinking and writing about the CPI and its legacy for at least 17 years and wanted to tell the story of how I thought it had shaped the political economy of the last century. Suddenly the CPI's centennial was almost upon us and I found myself with a potential window of time during which I might write such a book. During its writing, as if to exemplify the argument I had undertaken to advance, Trump won the Republican party nomination as presidential candidate and then the US presidential election. Consequently, writing these last two chapters has been somewhat like announcing a sporting event at which all the rules had been thrown out in a game nobody ever really understood in the first place. The aim of argument was to describe the development and global diffusion of rhetorical techniques that were first designed to unify a nation of rancorously disunited groups of people under a common cause; "sell" the idea that the United States was superior, morally, materially, and technically; and "sell" the idea that it needed to join a war in Europe to 'keep the world safe for democracy', as Wilson put it in his April 2, 1917 war speech. For some years up to that point, rhetoric had been "converted" to science under the heading of pragmatic philosophy, and so the rhetorical techniques used to achieve Wilson's war aims were undertaken and presented as science rather than rhetoric. The techniques subsequently underwent a century of analysis, testing, and refinement as if they were scientific. Alongside the scientific refinements of mass persuasion, new means of communication were developed, improved, deployed, and tested in the most "applied" ways possible on an international scale. WWII was a radio war. Vietnam was fought and lost on television. The current "War on Terror" is being fought out through internet channels.

Refined rhetorical techniques were taken up by corporations and governments throughout the world, disseminated through business schools, then through many high schools. Later, especially accelerating through the

1980s and 1990s, the techniques would follow in the path of strategic man-agement which had become part of almost every organisation in the West, large and small, public and private. Corporations, governments, universi-ties, and schools would all develop vision, mission, and values statements, five-year strategic plans, brand values, along with all things strategic and managerial (Graham, 2001). It was as if we were all at war.

Advertising principles have been taught to the very young under rubrics of critical literacy for decades, even for children in grade school, with the aim of pointing out the inner workings of mass persuasion in order to inocu-late the young. Children would no longer be the sleepy dupes of Madison Avenue; they would be critically armed against consumer culture and its oppressive ways. It was all a part of the progressive vision laid out a century before by the likes of Wilson, Dewey, Taylor, Lippmann, Wallas, Welles, Watson, and the Webbs. Alas, like most revolutionary discourse before and after, the progressive doctrine became orthodoxy, its cosmopolitanism became *de rigeur* for pedagogy and policy alike. Corporatism found a way to use it during globalisation. The once profoundly social and socialistic aims of the American Progressives gave way to individualistic emphases under the anti-socialist rhetoric that gained mightily from Creel's censor-ship, from corporatist discourse, and from a sense that "the public" and its opinion were fictions. Under the weight of big data, the almighty individual has been crowned as a "demographic of one", the symbol of a bespoke consumer society in an age of alleged "neoliberalism", which is anything but liberal.

Discourses of a market-based unity, along with a universal cosmopolitan "tolerance", peaked during the brief era of "globalisation", an ultimately nonsensical term that meant freedom for global corporatism, but not much at all for either the middle or working classes, even less for the billions of poor who would be enlisted in the ranks of cheap, "outsoured" labour. The attacks of September 11, 2001 spelled the end of globalisation. A painful return to nationalism ensued through a path of new and strange international coalitions, beginning with the "coalition of the willing", the members of which in 2003 pitched in to invade Iraq based on what would later prove to be false intelligence, and culminating in ultimate strangeness with the recent high-profile 'bromance' between the presidents of Russia and the United States (Graham, 2014). Somewhere in the middle of all that, in 2008, the global financial system collapsed, the trigger being the bankruptcy of Lehman Brothers, then worth $639 billion. In what could be seen as an attitudinal reversal of the Sherman Anti-Trust Act of the previous century, corporations that had helped create the crisis through a combination of neg-ligent and illegal practices were deemed "too big to fail" by governments in the United States and Europe. National and international treasuries were subsequently emptied into corporate coffers to prop up ailing and failing mega-corporations that had been playing fast and loose with mystical financial instruments nobody really understood (Graham, 2006). Only in Iceland and Ireland were corrupt bankers jailed. Australia avoided the worst of the effects by implementing Keynesian policies and freezing larger bank deposits. For the rest of the world, the financial collapse triggered austerity measures that would lead to the most rapid growth in wealth for the richest one per cent of humanity in recorded history.

Somewhere around the time Iraq was being invaded, MySpace and LinkedIn opened their virtual doors for business. Using the scaled-up capacities of what was called broadband internet, people could develop an online personal "profile" using photographs, music, text, and other multimedia. The new social media extended the logic of usenet groups to include live, mass interaction. In 2005, broadband developments made YouTube possible, a service that permitted public uploading and streaming of videos. Within a year, it had been sold for more than $1 billion. It launched under the legend "Broadcast Yourself". Any individual with broadband access to the internet could suddenly have his or her own global television network. Number one at the time of writing is PewDiePie (Felix Kjellberg of Sweden) who has 52 million subscribers and 3,083 videos which have been streamed 14 billion times, an audience more than 14 times that of any television broadcast in history. The service itself has a billion unique users, 300 hours of video are uploaded every minute as of October 2016, and its users collectively watch on average 323 days' worth of video each minute (DMR, 2017).

Twitter launched in 2006. We have seen now that it is a politically decisive platform. It has far fewer users than either Facebook or YouTube, 340 million active monthly users at the time of writing, 23 million of which are thought by Twitter management to be algorithms. Eighty-three per cent of world leaders use the platform, and roughly a quarter of its users are journalists. Eighty per cent of users access the platform by mobile phone. Katy Perry has the largest Twitter audience with 87 million "followers" (Smith, 2016).

Facebook has the largest social media user base with 1.79 billion users. That figure allegedly includes 83 million fake profiles. A total of 4.75 billion 'pieces of content' are shared by its users each day, including 510,000 comments, 293,000 status updates, and 136,000 photos (Zephoria, 2017). Social media marketers, Meltwater, claim that Facebook is good for brand storytelling, whereas Twitter is good for short bursts of information, the fastest way of getting news out, and is 'the Usain Bolt' of social media (Robinson, 2016). Some new media research suggests that YouTube hosts 'more self-promotional brand-related' material than Facebook or Twitter (Robinson, 2016).

Burgess and Green (2009) suggest that the social networking function of YouTube is potentially as important as its self-promotional function (p. 29). Focusing on social media in relative isolation has led other social media researchers to notice there is not one public but many, thus rediscovering what Lippmann, Dewey, Lasswell, and many others knew by the 1920s (Jansen, 2012). With 83 per cent of world leaders using it, and 25 per cent of its users being journalists, and being the "Usain Bolt" of social media, Twitter is the most strategic choice for would-be political conquistadors to tap into the main stream of television news media, which is still the most popular source of news worldwide, along with internet sites for print publications (Newman, Fletcher, Levy, and Nielsen, 2016).

A century after Creel, we are none the wiser in terms of understanding the relationships among our media environments, public opinion, and public action in any scientific sense. Given what we know about successful manipulation of the system to the point at which it can be used by an individual to gain command of the world's most powerful military by leveraging the impulses and principles of entertainment, we can safely say such processes are thoroughly rhetorical, that they are forms of social and political action rather than mere representations or socialisations, and in the current context that the requirements for successful political manipulation of the media environment do not include facts or even intelligence. What it does require is a critical sense of pieties and how to transgress upon them, which is to say, an acute sense of propriety and how to publicly trample it in such a way as to provoke outrage at a level that can attract mass media attention.

We must also understand that democracy is not a matter of fact. Certain facts are necessary to conduct the kinds of discussions required for some democratic decisions. But such facts do not include whether or not the crowds for Trump's inauguration were bigger than Obama's, or whether the media were merely in possession of 'alternative facts' to those of the Trump administration (Swayne, 2017). In a new twist to the "fake news" theme of the months leading up to the US election, Trump's first day in office was dominated by front-page discussions about the size of the inauguration crowds in front of the Lincoln Memorial and the concept of "alternative facts". It was also marked by 'the nation's biggest political demonstrations since the Vietnam war'. His administration claimed that 'record numbers of people' had attended the inauguration event, despite all evidence to the contrary. Spicer, Trump's Press Secretary, 'used his first White House briefing to shout at journalists', accusing them of 'deliberately false reporting' and issuing vague threats about holding them accountable for 'shameful and wrong' behaviour (Swayne, 2017). Later, senior Trump advisor Kellyanne Conway said Spicer was simply 'offering "alternative facts"' about events (Swayne, 2017). The blatant lying set off a wildfire of reaction across social and main stream media. Almost entirely unnoticed, news was announced of Congressional Bill *H.R.193—American Sovereignty Restoration Act of 2017* sponsored by Republican Mike D. Rogers, the purpose of which to repeal 'the United Nations Participation Act of 1945 and other specified related laws'.

> The bill requires: (1) the President to terminate U.S. membership in the United Nations (U.N.), including any organ, specialized agency, commission, or other formally affiliated body; and (2) closure of the U.S. Mission to the United Nations.
> The bill prohibits: (1) the authorization of funds for the U.S. assessed or voluntary contribution to the U.N., (2) the authorization of funds for any U.S. contribution to any U.N. military or peacekeeping operation, (3) the expenditure of funds to support the participation of U.S. Armed Forces as part of any U.N. military or peacekeeping operation, (4) U.S. Armed Forces from serving under U.N. command, and (5) diplomatic immunity for U.N. officers or employees.
>
> (United States Congress, 2017)

If the bill passes into law, Wilson's institutional legacy aimed at lasting global peace stands to be swept away.

Democracy is a moral project. It is about deciding what we ought and ought not do. It is about understanding what we mean when we use terms like "equality" and "freedom". It is not a project about facts or science, although both can help in reaching decisions about what actions to take on such matters as environmental destruction, infrastructure planning, and the development of new tools. But science cannot tell us what is good and right. That most central aspect of democracy is a project about competing interests and the competing opinions that pertain to those interests. Because it is a moral project, it is about future action and thus about choice. Because it is a project about choice, it is a project that involves constant persuasion. Democracy is therefore rhetorical and not susceptible to scientific control or analysis. It is quite possible for the general belief to prevail that the world is flat, that it was created in seven days, or that it is at the centre of the universe, and still have a healthy, functioning democracy. But democracy cannot function when trivial facts become the focus of partisan outrage, while a remote and unaccountable power elite acts without oversight, responsibility, or accountability in its own narrow interests.

A Brand "You" Day

Issues of strategic communication are an entirely novel affair in today's media environment. In her latest effort to attain YouTube stardom, Lena

Nersesian has promised to produce a sex tape for her audience as soon as she gets 1 million subscribers to her channel. Audience reactions are mixed (Roberts, 2017). Another ex-*Big Brother* reality television "star", Sam Pepper, again in search of increased subscriptions, staged a fake kidnapping of his friend who was then tied up and forced to watch a video of another friend being executed by a shot to the head, all of which was faked but clearly traumatic for the kidnapped boy who was not in on the "joke". "Facebook Live" has added a whole new set of possibilities to the "free flow of information". On December 30, 2016, 12-year-old Katelyn Davis live streamed her suicide to Facebook. It was a 40-minute video during which she described familial sexual abuse, apologised to her viewers, and then hung herself from a tree. Facebook took two weeks to begin removing copies of the video (Beck, 2017). That video followed closely on the heels of another Facebook Live feed of four friends torturing a disabled man. Korryn Gaines used Facebook Live to stream an armed standoff with Baltimore Police (Beck, 2017). On January 24, 2017, three men gang raped a woman in a three-hour, live-to-Facebook stream from Uppsala, Sweden (Sharman, 2017). There are early indications that the rape was conducted as part of an ongoing strategic communication campaign by Islamic radicals.

Strategic use of social media has been essential to the group known as ISIS, ISIL, and Islamic State. The group has been instrumental in confusing a previously clear-cut agenda in Syria aimed at removing the Assad regime following the rapid bloom and die off of the long forgotten "Arab Spring" of 2011. *Wired* (2016) ran a feature in April 2016 describing the strategy the group is using to 'win the social media war'. It consists of five parts: 'cultivate the brand' (increase "brand values" by reinforcing 'Westerners' perception of the Islamic State and its devotees as ruthless beyond comprehension'); 'innovate across platforms' (for example, instead of just showing a young man setting off to a suicide bombing, have a drone follow him to his destiny); 'crowdsource the distribution' (in other words, get it to go viral using opinion leaders and algorithmic triggers, such as 'Facebook's suicide flow'); 'inspire real-world action' ('manipulate Western nations into committing "cultural annihilation"'; get people to commit acts of violence and recruit others to the cause), and 'steer the conversation' (called "agenda setting" in the communication literature, in the case of social media 'crowdsource' individuals to generate favourable stories). This is social media's "AIDA" model, an acronym for the process of using advertising copy to stimulate Attention, Interest, Desire, and Action that comes down to us from Elias Lewis in the early 20th century and remains current in theory and practice today.

As plain technique, the elements of ISIL's strategy, those of advertising, and those of public relations are devoid of inherent moral weighting.

Strategic communication is a bundle of techniques for persuasion, for meeting organisational objectives, for aligning members with brand values, for aligning resources 'to deliver a common core message':

> Strategic communication entails packaging a core message that reflects an agency's overall strategy, values, purpose, and mission to persuade key stakeholders and enhance positioning. Active, not reactive, it establishes organizational clarity and dissuades freelance endeavors that may serve a few well, but detract from the organization's overall direction and purpose. To this end, one important tool, a solid strategic communication plan (SCP), should synchronize organizational units and align resources to deliver a common core message.
>
> (Hoover, 2010)

There is a moral vacuum at the core of these sorts of definitions. They can be found everywhere and be applied to absolutely anything. The description immediately above is a statement by the US Federal Bureau of Investigation (FBI). It could be for any organisation with any kind of purpose at all. It doesn't say what it wants to 'persuade key stakeholders' of, or what it wants them to identify with in order to 'enhance positioning'. It's not even as if the FBI had any competition to "position" itself against.

Such is the degree of moral vacuity in matters of strategy today. The basic enmities implied by strategic communication, and its close counterpart, strategic management, have been insinuated through every pore of society, regardless of whether there are enemies to deal with or not. Patricia Swann tells us that it is important for district schools to have an 'effective' website to help them reach their 'organizational goals' (2006, p. 24). She offers 'suggestions for developing a strategic communication approach for school district websites' which contain the same kinds of general and vacuous statements as the FBI's statement, the DoD's now abandoned strategic communication plan, and the millions of other plans like it, from Raytheon's corporate responsibility statements to the strategic communication approaches of Oxfam, the International Red Cross, and Save the Children Fund (Dijkzeul and Moke, 2005). Surkov's approach in Russia is a parody of the West's strategic communication approach, parodied by Surkov for its ability to flatten out any kind of critical edge and demolish the possibility of definition:

> "Effective manager," a term quarried from Western corporate speak, is transmuted into a term to venerate the president as the most "effective manager" of all. "Effective" becomes the raison d'être for everything: Stalin was an "effective manager" who had to make sacrifices for the sake of being "effective." The words trickle into the streets:

"Our relationship is not effective" lovers tell each other when they break up. "Effective," "stability": No one can quite define what they actually mean, and as the city transforms and surges, everyone senses things are the very opposite of stable, and certainly nothing is "effective," but the way Surkov and his puppets use them the words have taken on a life of their own and act like falling axes over anyone who is in any way disloyal.

(Pomerantsev, 2014)

Surkov's strategy for destabilising reality is no different to that of psychological operations in the US military, a bundle of techniques for 'climbing inside' every movement in Russia in order to control it, just as the US military psyops techniques are based on 'getting inside the enemy's . . . decision-making mechanism' (Oliver, 2009, p. 63). While the US military is restricted in its domain of operations to foreign soil, corporations are not. Keith Oliver (2009) exhorts business people to promote their organisations 'the Marine Corps way' and offers the principles of military 'strategic communication' ('Ahhhh, the paradigm du jour') to the corporate world, and anybody else who cares to read his book, for use wherever they wish. Technique is uncontrollable.

A Plea for Rhetoric

A controversy is normally an exploitation of a systematic set of misunderstandings for war-like purposes.

—Richards (1936, p. 39)

The Creel century could be described from one point of view as the mass industrialisation of military propaganda and the subsequent diffusion of its tools and techniques on a global scale, down to the level of the individual. At another, it could be seen in Neil Postman's framing as the total entertainmentisation of political, cultural, and social life. Or it could be seen as total militarisation, the successful instigation of an endless war of all against all for the resources of the Earth: perfect competition. It could also be seen as the culmination of a long reaction to the breakdown of feudalism and its re-establishment in a new, anonymous corporate form. Or it could be seen simply as the longest, biggest, and most violent robbery in human history. It all depends how you frame it. The perspective I have presented here is informed by a sensitivity to the vast differences between the language of fact and the language of exhortation. Formally the two "look" very different. Functionally, though, they blur into and displace each other. The long history of language arts that begins in ancient Greece and continues in an almost unbroken way up to today centres around rhetoric, dialectic, grammar, and poetics. Among all of those, rhetoric was the medium of democracy from the earliest times. Plato begins what would be a long fought assault against rhetoric's emotive, opinionated aspects in favour of logic, reason, and rationality (Dryzek, 2010; Havelock, 1963).

Plato also set in train the long quest for perfect knowledge of the world, a world in which representation would mirror reality, making him perhaps the first scientist of record. The urge to scientism and its refinement over centuries gave great technical rewards to humanity in general, bringing with it abundant food, rapid transport, longer life, and seemingly infinite control over our environment. It also brought destructive power only dreamed of in the most fevered apocalyptic visions. With scientism came serial attempts to cleanse language of its various "biases", from Plato, to Bentham, to Korzybski and Hayakawa, to the latest algorithmic studies in neuro-linguistic programming, the idea that language could be rendered neutral and objective, a mirror of reality, has never been far away. Yet as Malinowski showed us at the beginning of this book, we first learn to communicate by getting people to do things for us, to feed us, clothe us, comfort us. Our first actions on the world are done through others. Our earliest lessons in communication are therefore rhetorical, emotive, and viscerally motivated towards control of our social scene. We continue those applied lessons today in a globally interconnected "classroom" of unprecedented rhetorical intensity and mass.

And yet we have all but abandoned two and a half millennia of knowledge about what rhetoric is, how it works on people, what it does to us, and how to practice it productively for the general good. What was for centuries the basis of all education is now confined largely to composition studies and some areas of organisational communication, public relations, and linguistics. As it turns out, it may well be that the relegation of facts to a much more minor role in our civic discussions is required in order to make space for discussion of social goods and the consequences of our words. "Progress" is meaningless if it is not progress towards something. "Conservatism" is just as meaningless a term if we are not clear about what it is we aim to conserve. I am not suggesting that reintroducing scholastic modes of rhetorical instruction would cure all our political and social ills, or even that such an approach is possible given the degree of specialisation that we have achieved. However, as a grounding for both general and specialised education, a sensitivity to the rhetorical—the persuasive—ought to be built into the earliest years of our education as citizens if we are ever to break out of the current morass.

Even more importantly, we must come to understand our words as actions rather than information, as always working upon the world to some effect, even if it is only upon ourselves. That goes to a far broader agenda, well beyond rhetoric for its own sake, into the moral dimensions of our lives, into purposes and motivations, into deliberation about our collective future as a species, and most especially into how we see the world and understand the limits of our perception. If nothing else, a revived rhetoric ought to be a better way to do battle over the most important aspects of our being than the current modes of interaction that extend from blatant advertising to the kinds of "messaging" conducted through the extreme violence and "collective punishments" of Total War. Admiral Michael Mullen (2009) has this to say about strategic communication and the nature of "the message" in current circumstances:

> It is time for us to take a harder look at "strategic communication."
>
> Frankly, I don't care for the term. We get too hung up on that word, *strategic*. If we've learned nothing else these past 8 years, it should be that the lines between strategic, operational, and tactical are blurred beyond distinction. This is particularly true in the world of communication, where videos and images plastered on the Web . . . can and often do drive national security decision making.
>
> The problem isn't that we are bad at communicating or being outdone by men in caves. Most of them aren't even in caves. The Taliban and al Qaeda live largely among the people. They intimidate and control and communicate from within, not from the sidelines.
>
> And they aren't just out there shooting videos, either. They deliver. Want to know what happens if somebody violates their view of Sharia law? You don't have to look very far or very long. Each beheading, each bombing, and each beating sends a powerful message or, rather, *is* a powerful message.
>
> (Mullen, 2009)

Human communion is not about "sending a message". That is the method of dictatorship and confuses intimidation with communication, and authoritarianism with democratic governance. It is a variant of the political and corporate crisis strategy that says, when things don't go as planned in terms of opinion, public reaction, or collective public failure, the remedy is "to communicate the message more clearly to our stakeholders"; or that "we need to get our message out there", even if that means bombing a whole country "back to the stone age", as Curtis LeMay expressed his preferred approach to communicating with North Vietnam at one point. The constant resort to "sending a message" indicates a breakdown in our understanding of the very nature of communication; a childish and unconscious return to a "silver bullet" theory in the assumption that a witless public has simply misunderstood what we were up to. Even the strategic imperative to "communicate a core message", or to constantly communicate "brand values" for an organisation is an act of censorship and aggression aimed at shutting down alternative meanings, understandings, negotiations, and objections that will happen whether we want them to or not.

At the other extreme is Surkov's, and seemingly Trump's, strategy of fostering misunderstanding and distraction on a gross scale; engineering mass confusion and obfuscation; of driving the public agenda through outrage, blatant incoherence, blatant lying, followed by blatant confessions that it was all really just a bit of a laugh.

> After spending a day defending the literal truth of his claim that President Obama was "the founder" of ISIS, Donald Trump switched course on Friday, claiming it was an instance of misunderstood "sarcasm." . . . In an early-morning tweet Trump, the Republican nominee for president, said the media misreported his remarks and "didn't get sarcasm." . . . Trump added that the media were intentionally twisting his words and called them "the lowest forms of humanity."
>
> (Bahl, 2016)

I. A. Richards (1936) argues that rhetoric 'should be a study of misunderstanding and its remedies' (p. 3). He defines the most basic problems of understanding in much the same way Lippmann (1922) describes our various networks of 'stereotypes', and what Burke (1966) calls 'terministic screens'. Richards uses the term 'contexts' to describe the same problematic phenomena, the very nature of all our words, which are always contradictory abstractions, shorthands for the many unique events of reality that we must somehow gather up under names of one sort or another if we are to understand and communicate with each other. Our language is given to us; each of us emerges into it as a framework for making sense of our world. In that sense it could be seen to have a life of its own of which we are just a part. Having emerged from millennia of organic development among people seeking to survive and thrive, never settled or still, often reversing the shared senses of their own meanings over time, our words filter reality for us, sorting it into pregiven, abstract categories (Richards, 1936, pp. 29–37).

Yet none of that is to suggest we can never trust our meanings, just that they are always active, open to negotiation and "on the move", or at least they should be. Richards (1936) argues that 'the whole business of Rhetoric comes down to comparisons between the meanings of words' (p. 37). That is not to say we need to engage in endless analysis over every term, which is currently what happens each time public figures tell blatant lies, but it is just to constantly remind ourselves that each of us responds to a set of terms from a unique and partial point of view that changes with everything from mood to time of day to where we are. We face an infinitely large and complex universe with a very limited vocabulary. Presently our public political logic has been reduced to that which was called by Aristotle '*sophisticus elenchis*, its matter premises that seem to be generally accepted or appropriate, but really are not, discussed by "those who argue as competitors and rivals to the death" seeking by whatever means to refute the opponent' (Joseph, 1947, p. 19). Because democracy is about what we ought to do and how we ought to do it, its most important matters are matters of opinion, not fact. As such, rhetoric and dialectic are the linguistic counterparts of democracy. Science is of limited help.

It could be that we are entering the darkest of dark ages. As I put the finishing touches to this manuscript, Trump has decreed that the date of his inauguration shall hereafter be known as 'National Day of Patriotic Devotion' (Kearns, 2017). In his first two days as president, Trump has placed a gag on employees of the Environmental Protection Agency, rescinded the Affordable Care Act, and banned funding to foreign aid groups who discuss abortion as part of family planning. His list of cabinet nominees is filled with contrarians and inexperienced partisans. In an historical irony, he has nominated Rex Tillerson, immediate past CEO of ExxonMobil, as Secretary of State. ExxonMobil is a direct descendant of Rockefeller's Standard Oil. The ongoing wars being fought in the Middle East are wars for control of oil, and Trump has said publicly that the United States should have 'taken Iraq's oil' to stop ISIS but that now 'we'll have another chance' (in Hartmann, 2017).

I might well have named this book *The Progressive Century*, since it has Progressive Era politics to thank for most of its defining themes, including socialism and the attacks on it, the idea of an American Century, the idea that our political lives should be conducted according to scientific standards, that public opinion is the most important element in the management of mass democracy, and that it can be managed scientifically. It is the century in which work would finally be organised scientifically, along with public opinion, thought, and behaviour. Lippmann coined 'manufacture of consent' as a critical term for the damage he saw that the CPI had done during WWI. His was also a plea for dialogue, for education. The foil against rule by specialisation is a reimagined general education, and the most general education we can give is in the language arts.

At the end of the Creel century, the world is fragmenting at every level. The impending US withdrawal from the UN, Britain's exit from the European Union, and even long-standing separatisms like the ones being fought out in Spain mark the continued fragmenting of political alliances that have been in varying degrees of turmoil since the "War to end all wars" 100 years ago. That war began a push to unite the world in peace, first through the efforts of The Inquiry which would help establish The League of Nations and, later, the UN. The broadcast era made mass societies possible. People could be "spoken to" and commune in their millions, all at the same time, instilling a feeling of community, setting agendas for deliberation and consideration on a mass scale, and providing a means, on the one hand, of democratic checks led by an ideally independent press, and on the other, for unprecedented levels of state control in cases where public dissent had been outlawed and ownership of influence centralised. Today the masses are no longer, at least not in any centrally mediated sense. If there is to be a peace today, it cannot be interpartisan; it must be interpersonal. It cannot be based on group settlements; it must be a settlement among individuals. Tomorrow, January 25, 2017, the Great Wall of Mexico is to be introduced into law, and the United States is legislating to halt 'a decades-old program that grants refuge to the world's most vulnerable people' (Davis and Haberman, 2017). Tomorrow marks the end of Progress.

References

ABC. (2017, January 15). Donald Trump's inauguration: Who is (and isn't) perform-ing? *Australian Broadcasting Corporation* (ABC). Available online at: www.abc.net.au/news/2017-01-14/who-is-and-isnt-attending-the-donald-trump-inauguration/8180122

Adams, H. C. (1902). What is publicity? *The Northern Review*, *175* (553): 895–904.

Allcott, H. and Gentzkow, M. (2017). Social media and fake news in the 2016 elec-tion. *Stanford University*. Available online at: https://web.stanford.edu/~gentzkow/research/fakenews.pdf

Allen, F. E. (2012). Sarbanes-Oxley 10 years later: Boards are still the problem. *Forbes*. Available online at: www.forbes.com/sites/frederickallen/2012/07/29/sarbanes-oxley-10-years-later-boards-are-still-the-problem/#6a4fa2ccd851

Alvarez, M. (2005). The origins of the film exchange. *Film History*, *17* (4): 431–465.

Amity University. (2016). *Amity College of Corporate Warfare*. Uttar Pradesh, India. Available online at: www.amity.edu/accw/default.htm. Accessed October 17, 2016.

Appell, D. (2007, May 28). Assets near $25 trillion. *Pensions and Investments Online*. Available online at: http://www.pionline.com/.

Aristotle, A. (1991). *The art of rhetoric* (Trans. H. C. Lawson-Tancred). London: Penguin Classics.

Auerbach, J. D. (2015). *Weapons of democracy: Propaganda, progressivism, and American public opinion*. Baltimore, MD: Johns Hopkins University Press.

Austin, J. L. (1962). *How to do things with words*. Cambridge, MA: Harvard Uni-versity Press.

Bahl, A. (2016, August 13). Trump discovers the media can't take a joke when it comes to Obama and ISIS. *Yahoo News*. Available online at: www.yahoo.com/news/trump-discovers-media-t-joke-000000304.html.

Baker, P. (2017, January 17). Trump entering White House unbent and unpopular. *New York Times*. Available online at: www.nytimes.com/2017/01/17/us/politics/donald-trump-obama-approval-rating.html.

Balaghi, S. (2002). *The double-bind of Americans of Middle Eastern heritage*. New York, NY: The Kevorkian Center, New York University. Available online at: www.nyu.edu/gsas/program/neareast/911_resources/essay_balaghi.html. Accessed August 30, 2002.

Barnard, C. I. (1938). *The functions of the executive*. Cambridge, MA: Harvard Uni-versity Press.

Barry, A. (2016). Television, truth and democracy. *Media, Culture & Society*, *15* (3): 487–496.

Bartlett, D. L. and Steele, J. B. (2007, March). Washington's $8 billion shadow. *Vanity Fair*, 342–358.

Bates, L. (2017, January 18). 'Ugly women don't sell burgers'—the trickle-down effect of Team Trump. *The Guardian*. Available online at: www.theguardian.com/ us-news/2017/jan/18/trickle-down-effect-team-trumps-labour-secretary-nomi nee-andrew-puzder.

Beattie, J. (2017, January 16). World's 8 richest men are now worth as much as half the world's population. *The Mirror*. Available online at: www.mirror.co.uk/news/ world-news/top-eight-richest-men-worth-9629700.

Beck, L. (2017, January 16). A 12-year-old girl live-streamed her suicide and it took Facebook 2 weeks to remove it. *Cosmopolitan*. Available online at: www.cosmo politan.com/lifestyle/a8603218/12-year-old-girl-live-streamed-her-suicide-and-it-took-facebook-2-weeks-to-remove-it/.

Beech, E. (2014, April 30). U.S. government says it lost $11.2 billion on GM bailout. *Reuters*. Available online at: www.reuters.com/article/us-autos-gm-treasury-idUSBREA3T0MR20140430.

Bender, J. (2015). Here are all the problems with the F-35 that the Pentagon found in a 2014 report. *Business Insider Australia*. Available online at: www.businessin sider.com.au/here-are-all-the-problems-with-the-f-35-that-the-pentagon-found-in-a-2014-report-2015-3.

Bentham, J. (1824). *The book of fallacies from unfinished papers of Jeremy Bentham*. London: J. and H. L. Hunt.

Bernays, E. (1928). *Propaganda*. Brooklyn, NY: IG Publishing.

Bernays, E. (1923). *Crystallising public opinion*. Brooklyn, NY: IG Publishing.

The Big Smoke. (2016). About us. *The Big Smoke*. Sydney, Australia: The Belleford Group. Available online at: http://thebigsmoke.com.au/about-us/. Accessed Oct 16, 2016.

Bloch, M. (1962). *Feudal society*. London: Routledge & Kegan Paul.

Bloomberg News. (2007, September 11). Consumer Credit Slowed in July. *The New York Times*. Available at http://www.nytimes.com/2007/09/11/business/11econ.html.

Bourdieu, P. (1998). *Practical reason: On the theory of practice*. London: Polity.

Bourdieu, P. (1990). *The logic of practice* (Trans. R. Nice). London: Polity.

Brady, K. (1984). *Ida Tarbell: Portrait of a muckraker*. New York, NY: Putnam.

Brewer, S. A. (2009). *Why America fights: Patriotism and war propaganda from the Philippines to Iraq*. London: Oxford University Press.

Brown, F. J. (1937). Media of propaganda. *Journal of Educational Sociology*, *10* (6): 323–330.

Brown, J. (2003). The anti-propaganda tradition in the United States. *The Public Diplo-macy Alumni Association*. Available online at: www.publicdiplomacy.org/19.htm.

Bullard, A. (1917). *Mobilising America*. New York: The Macmillan Company.

Bullock, A. (1991). *Hitler and Stalin: Parallel lives*. London: Fontana.

Burgess, J. E. and Green, J. B. (2009). *YouTube: Online video and participatory culture*. Cambridge: Digital Media & Society; Polity Press.

Burke, K. (1966). *Language as symbolic action: Essays on life, literature, and method*. Berkeley, CA: University of California Press.

Burke, K. (1961). *The rhetoric of religion: Studies in logology.* Berkeley, CA: University of California Press.

Burke, K. (1950/1969). *A rhetoric of motives.* Berkeley, CA: University of California Press.

Burke, K. (1945/1962). *A grammar of motives.* Berkeley, CA: University of California Press.

Burke, K. (1942). War and cultural life. *American Journal of Sociology, 48* (3): 404–410.

Burke, K. (1937/1984). *Attitudes toward history.* Berkeley, CA: University of California Press.

Burke, K. (1935/1984). *Permanence and change: An anatomy of purpose.* Berkeley, CA: University of California Press.

Caldwell, L. (2017, January 20). Trump's defense and homeland security picks sworn-in. *NBC News.* Available online at: www.nbcnews.com/storyline/inauguration-2017/senate-confirms-gen-james-mattis-defense-secretary-n710061

Callahan, R. E. (1962). *Education and the cult of efficiency: A study of the social forces that have shaped the administration of the public schools.* Chicago, IL: University of Chicago Press.

Campbell, B. C. (2014). *The growth of American government.* Bloomington, IN: Indiana University Press.

Carey, J. (1997). *James Carey: A critical reader* (Eds. E. S. Munson and C. A. Warren). Minneapolis, MN: University of Minnesota Press.

Carey, J. (1989). *Communication as culture: Essays on media and society.* New York: Routledge.

Carnegie, D. (1937). *How to win friends and influence people.* New York, NY: Cornerstone Publishing.

Casson, H. N. (1911). *Ads and sales: A study of advertising and selling from the standpoint of the new principles of scientific management.* Chicago, IL: McClurg and Sons.

Cawsey, S. F. (1999). Royal eloquence, royal propaganda, and the use of the sermon in the Medieval crown of Aragon c. 1200–1410. *Journal of Ecclesiastical History, 50* (3): 442–463.

Cazden, C., Cope, B., Fairclough, N., Luke, A., Luke, C., et al. (New London Group). (1996). A pedagogy of multiliteracies: Designing social futures. *Harvard Educational Review, 66* (1): 60–92.

CDI. (1997). *The military in the movies* [documentary transcript]. Available online at: www.cdi.org/adm/Transcripts/1020/

Chadwick, S. (2014, June 19). For Sony and Coke, the real World Cup challenge is the battle for 6 billion eyeballs. *The Conversation.* Available online at: http://theconversation.com/for-sony-and-coke-the-real-world-cup-challenge-is-the-battle-for-6-billion-eyeballs-28175

Charlton, A. (2016, August 8). Economist Dr Andrew Charlton discusses the RBA's latest interest rate cut. *The 7.30 Report.* Sydney: Australian Broadcasting Corporation (ABC). Available online at: www.abc.net.au/7.30/content/2016/s4512076.htm. Accessed August 8, 2016.

Cohen, M. (2015). As VIP play shrinks and shifts, Morgan Stanley upbeat on global gaming. *Forbes.* Available online at: www.forbes.com/sites/muhammadcohen/

2015/04/07/as-vip-play-shrinks-and-shifts-morgan-stanley-upbeat-on-global-gaming/#6a64d59d122e.

Cone, S. (2005). Pulling the plug on America's propaganda: Sen. J.W. Fulbright's leadership of the anti-propaganda movement, 1943–74. *Journalism History, 30* (4): 166–177.

Cooley, C. H. (1909). *Social organization: A study of the larger mind.* New York, NY: Charles Scribner's Sons.

Coughlan, S. (2017, January 17). What does post-truth mean for a philosopher? *British Broadcasting Corporation (BBC)*. Available online at: www.bbc.com/news/education-38557838.

Creel, G. (1920). *How we advertised America: The first telling of the amazing story of the Committee on public information that carried the gospel of Americanism to every corner of the globe.* New York, NY and London: Harper and Brothers.

Curtis, A. (2016). Adam Curtis' new film HyperNormalisation to premiere on BBC iPlayer this October. *BBC Media Centre.* London: The BBC. Available online at: www.bbc.co.uk/mediacentre/latestnews/2016/adam-curtis-hypernormalisation.

Davenport, T. H. and Beck, J. C. (2001). *The attention economy: The new currency of business.* Boston, MA: Harvard Business School Press.

Davis, J. H. and Haberman, M. (2017, January 24). Trump expected to order Mexican border wall. *New York Times.* Available online at: www.nytimes.com/2017/01/24/us/politics/wall-border-trump.html.

Davies, W. (2017, January 19). How statistics lost their power—and why we should fear what comes next. *The Guardian.* Available online at: www.theguardian.com/politics/2017/jan/19/crisis-of-statistics-big-data-democracy

Dewey, J. (1903). Democracy in education. *The Elementary School Teacher, 4* (4): 193–204.

Diamond, J. (2016, January 24). Trump: I could 'shoot somebody and I wouldn't lose voters'. *Cable Network News (CNN)*. Available online at: http://edition.cnn.com/2016/01/23/politics/donald-trump-shoot-somebody-support/.

Dijkzeul, D. and Moke, M. (2005). Public communication strategies of international humanitarian organizations. *International Review of the Red Cross, 87* (860): 673–691.

Dixon, T. (1996). *Communication, organisation, and performance.* New Jersey: Ablex.

Drury, I., Williams, D. and Greenhill, S. (2011, May 4). *Obama watched Bin Laden die on live video as shoot-out beamed to White House.* Available online at: www.dailymail.co.uk/news/article-1382859/Osama-bin-Laden-dead-Photo-Obama-watching-Al-Qaeda-leader-die-live-TV.html.

Dryzek, J. S. (2010). Rhetoric in democracy: A systemic appreciation. *Political Theory, 38* (3): 319–339.

Eco, U. (1989). Introduction. In C. K. Ogden and I. A. Richards (1923/1989). *The meaning of meaning.* Orlando, FL: Harcourt, Brace, and Janovich: v–xi.

The Economist. (2017). The global debt clock. *The Economist.* Available online at: www.economist.com/content/global_debt_clock.

The Economist. (1999). Standard ogre. *The Economist.* Available online at: www.economist.com/node/347251

Eisenhower, D. D. (1961). *Farewell radio and television address to the American people by President Dwight D. Eisenhower, January 17, 1961.* Kansas: The

Dwight D. Eisenhower Library. Available online at: www.eisenhower.archives. gov/farewell.htm

Erikson, R. S. and Wlezien, C. (2012). Markets vs. polls as election predictors: An historical assessment. *Electoral Studies*, *31*: 532–539.

Fahrenthold, D. A. (2016, October 8). Trump recorded having extremely lewd conversation about women in 2005. *The Washington Post*. Available online at: www.washingtonpost.com/politics/trump-recorded-having-extremely-lewd-conversation-about-women-in-2005/2016/10/07/3b9ce776-8cb4–11e6-bf8a-3d26847eeed4_story.html.

Fandos, N. (2015, January 15). Corporations open the cash spigot for Trump's inauguration. *New York Times*. Available online at: www.nytimes.com/2017/01/15/us/politics/trump-inauguration-donations-corporations.html.

Farmer, B. (2008). *American conservatism: History, theory and practice*. Cambridge: Cambridge Scholars Publishing.

Feldstein, M. (2006). A muckraking model: Investigative reporting cycles in American history. *The Harvard International Journal of Press/Politics*, *11* (2): 105–120.

Fike, C. E. (1959). The influence of the Creel Committee and the American Red Cross on Russian-American relations, 1917–1919. *The Journal of Modern History*, *31* (2): 93–109.

Friedman, T. L. (1999, March 28). A manifesto for the fast world. *New York Times Magazine*, pp. 40–44, 61, 70–71, 84, 96.

Gallup. (2016). *About Gallup*. Washington, D.C.: Gallup. Available online at http://www.gallup.com/corporate/178136/george-gallup.aspx

Gallup, G. (1938). Testing public opinion. *Public Opinion Quarterly*, *2* (1) [Special supplement: Public opinion in a democracy]: 8–14.

Gardner, D. (2008). *Risk: The science and politics of fear*. London: Virgin.

Gates, W. (2006, May 17). *Beyond Business Intelligence: Delivering a Comprehensive Approach to Enterprise Information Management*. Seatttle, WA: Microsoft Corporation. Available online at http://www.microsoft.com/mscorp/execmail/2006/05-17eim.mspx

Gilbert, H. F. (1917). Folk-Music in art-music – A discussion and a theory. *The Musical Quarterly, 3* (4): 577–601.

Graham, D. (2014, December 24). Donald Trump's hot-and-cold bromance with Vladimir Putin. *The Atlantic*. Available online at: www.theatlantic.com/politics/archive/2016/12/trump-putin-so-true/511679/.

Graham, P. (2016). Halliday and Lemke: A comparison of contextual potentials for two metafunctional systems. *Critical Discourse Studies*, *13* (5): 548–576.

Graham, P. (2006). *Hypercapitalism: Language, new media, and social perceptions of value*. New York, NY: Peter Lang Publishing.

Graham, P. (2002). Predication and propagation: A method for analysing evaluative meanings in technology policy. *TEXT*, *22* (2): 227–268.

Graham, P. (2001). Contradictions and institutional convergences: Genre as method. *Journal of Future Studies*, *5* (4): 1–30.

Graham, P. and Hearn, G. (2010). The digital dark ages: A retro-speculative history of possible futures. In C. Anton (Ed.), *Valuation and media ecology: Ethics, morals, and laws*. Cresskill, NJ: Hampton Press: 141–166.

Graham, P., Keenan, T. and Dowd, A. (2004). A call to arms at the end of history: A discourse-historical analysis of George W. Bush's declaration of war on terror. *Discourse & Society, 15* (2–3): 199–221.

Graham, P. and Luke, A. (2011). Critical discourse analysis and political economy of communication: Understanding the new corporate order. *Cultural Politics, 7* (1): 103–132.

Graham, P. and Luke, A. (2005). The language of neofeudal corporatism and the war on Iraq. *Journal of Language & Politics, 4* (1): 11–39.

Graham, P. and Luke, A. (2003). Militarising the body politic: New media as weapons of mass instruction. *Body and Society, 9* (4): 149–168.

Graham, P. and McKenna, B. J. (2000). A theoretical and analytical synthesis of autopoiesis and sociolinguistics for the study of organisational communication. *Social Semiotics, 10* (1): 41–59.

Gray, K. (2001, October). West Deptford students mourn the loss of attack victims. *The Talon*. West Deptford, NJ: West Deptford High School, p. 1.

Guardian. (2017, January 16). John Brennan: Trump's 'Nazi Germany' tweet to US agencies was 'outrageous'. *The Guardian*. Available online at: www.theguardian.com/us-news/2017/jan/15/john-brennan-trump-nazi-germany-russia.

Hallahan, K., Holtzhausen, D., Ruler, B. van, Verčič, D. and Sriramesh, K. (2007). Defining strategic communication. *International Journal of Strategic Communication, 1* (1): 3–35.

Halliday, M. A. K. (1994). *An introduction to functional grammar* (2nd ed.). London: Arnold.

Hartmann, M. (2017, January 22). Trump says U.S. should have stolen Iraq's oil, and 'Maybe we'll have another chance'. *New York Magazine*. Available online at: http://nymag.com/daily/intelligencer/2017/01/trump-u-s-may-get-another-chance-to-take-iraqi-oil.html

Havelock, E. A. (1986). *The muse learns to write: Reflections on orality and literacy from antiquity to the present.* New Haven, CT: Yale University Press.

Havelock, E. A. (1963). *Preface to Plato.* New Haven, CT: Yale University Press.

Hayakawa, S. I. (1941). *Language in action: A guide to accurate thinking reading and writing.* New York, NY: Harcourt Brace and Company.

Hayakawa, S. I. (1939). General semantics and propaganda. *The Public Opinion Quarterly, 3* (2): 197–208.

Hensch, M. (2017, January 4). Spicer: Trump's tweets 'drive the news'. *The Hill.* Available online at: http://thehill.com/homenews/administration/312775-spicer-trumps-tweets-drive-the-news.

Hesse, A. (2016, August 18). Trillions go missing from the Military: Pentagon can't account for $6.5T in taxpayer cash. *Fox News*. Available online at: http://nation.foxnews.com/2016/08/18/trillions-go-missing-military-pentagon-cant-account-65t-taxpayer-cash.

Hobbs, R. and McGee, S. (2014). Teaching about Propaganda: An Examination of the Historical Roots of Media Literacy. *Journal of Media Literacy Education, 6* (2): 56–67.

Hoover, C. (2010). *The strategic communication plan.* Washington, DC: US Federal Bureau of Investigation (FBI). Available online at: https://leb.fbi.gov/2010/august/the-strategic-communication-plan.

I Fucking Love Science (IFLS). (2017a). I Fucking Love Science teams up with The Science Channel to curate the best science content on the web. *Editor's Blog*. www.iflscience.com/editors-blog/i-fucking-love-science-teams-science-channel-curate-best-science-content-web/

IFLS. (2017b). Terms of use. *IFLS*. Available online at: www.iflscience.com/terms-of-use/

IFLS. (2017c). Blonde-haired moth with small genitals named after Donald Trump. *IFLS*. Available online at: www.iflscience.com/plants-and-animals/blondehaired-moth-with-small-genitals-named-after-donald-trump/

Ingram, M. (2015, August 13). The attention economy and the implosion of traditional media. *Fortune*. Available online at: http://fortune.com/2015/08/12/attention-economy/

James, W. (1907). *Pragmatism: A new name for some old ways of thinking*. New York, NY: Longmans Green.

Jansen, S. C. (2013). Semantic Tyranny: How Edward L. Bernays stole Walter Lippmann's mojo and got away with it and why it still matters. *International Journal of Communication*, 7: 1094–1111.

Jansen, S. C. (2012). *Walter Lippmann: A critical introduction to media and communication theory*. New York, NY: Peter Lang.

Jansen, S. C. (2009). Phantom conflict: Lippmann, Dewey, and the fate of the public in modern society. *Communication and Critical/Cultural Studies*, 6 (3): 221–245.

Joseph, M. Sr. (1947). *Shakespeare's use of the arts of language*. New York, NY: Columbia University Press.

Kearns, L. (2017, January 23). Trump proclaims his inauguration a 'National Day of Patriotic Devotion'. *The Huffington Post*. Available online at: www.huffingtonpost.com/entry/trump-national-day-of-patriotic-devotion_us_588681a9e4b0e3a7356b553d.

Kellner, D. (2004). 9/11, Spectacles of terror, and media manipulation: A critique of Jihadist and Bush media politics. *Critical Discourse Studies*, 1 (1): 41–64.

Kesher, P. J. (1990). John B. Watson at J. Walter Thompson: The legitimation of "Science" in advertising. *Journal of Advertising*, 19 (2): 49–59.

Killebrew, J. B. and Myrick, H. (1897). *Tobacco leaf, its culture and cure, marketing and manufacture: A practical handbook on the most approved methods in growing, harvesting, curing, packing and selling tobacco, also of tobacco manufacture*. New York, NY: Orange Judd Company.

Koehl, R. (1960). Feudal aspects of national socialism. *The American Political Science Review*, 54 (4): 921–933.

Lafollette, H. (2000). Pragmatic ethics. In Lafollette, H. & Persson, I. (Eds.). (2000). *The Blackwell guide to ethical theory*. London: Blackwell: 400–419.

Landers, J. (2013). Hearst's Magazine, 1912–1914: Muckraking sensationalist. *Journalism History*, 38 (4): 221–232.

Lasswell, H. D. (1972). Communications research and public policy. *Public Opinion Quarterly*, 36 (3): 301–310.

Lasswell, H. D. (1948/1960). The structure and function of communication in society. In W. Schramm (Ed.), *Mass Communications* (2nd ed.). Urbana, IL: University of Illinois Press.

Lasswell, H. D. (1941). World attention survey. *Public Opinion Quarterly*, 5 (3): 456–462.

Lasswell, H. D. (1938). *Propaganda technique in the World War.* New York, NY: Peter Smith.

Lasswell, H. D. (1927). The theory of political propaganda. *The American Political Science Review, 21* (3): 627–631.

Lazarsfeld, P. F. (1940). *Radio and the printed page: An introduction to the study of radio and its role in the communication of ideas.* New York, NY: Duell, Sloan, and Pearce.

Lee, P. (2016). *Materials for the history of statistics.* The University of York. Available online at: www.york.ac.uk/depts/maths/histstat/lies.htm.

Leetaru, K. (2017a). 2016 campaign television tracker. *GDELT Project.* Available online at: http://television.gdeltproject.org/cgi-bin/iatv_campaign2016/iatv_campaign2016.

Leetaru, K. (2017b). 2016 campaign web tracker. *GDELT Project.* Available online at: http://television.gdeltproject.org/cgi-bin/iatv_campaign2016/iatv_campaign2016_web?filter_candidate=&filter_timespan=ALL&filter_displayas=PERCENTALL

Leetaru, K. (2015, August 21). Is Donald Trump dominating media coverage of the Republican race? *The Guardian.* Available online at: www.theguardian.com/news/datablog/2015/aug/20/donald-trump-dominating-media-coverage.

Lemke, J. L. (1995). *Textual politics: Discourse and social dynamics.* London: Taylor & Francis.

Levingstone, I. (2016, July 28). Political polls vs betting markets: Here's why they conflict. *CNBC.* Available online at: www.cnbc.com/2016/07/28/political-polls-vs-betting-markets-heres-why-they-conflict.html

Lippman, W. (1922). *Public opinion.* New York, NY: W. W. Norton & Co.

Luhmann, N. (1995). *Social systems* (Trans. J. Bednarz, Jr. with D. Baecker). Stanford, CA: Stanford University Press.

McGeough, P. (2017, January 20). Twilight of the Trumps? What America can expect for the next four years. *Brisbane Times.* Available online at: www.brisbanetimes.com.au/world/twilight-of-the-trumps-what-america-can-expect-for-the-next-four-years-20170119-gtuxkz.html.

McLuhan, M. (1964). *Understanding media: The extensions of man.* London: Routledge.

Malinowski, B. (1923). Supplement I. In C. K. Ogden and I. A. Richards (1923/1989) (Eds.), *The meaning of meaning.* Orlando, FL: Harcourt, Brace, and Janovich: 296–396.

Maturana, H. and Varela, F. (1980). *Autopoiesis and cognition: The realisation of the living.* Dordrecht, Holland: Reidel.

Merkle, J. A. (1980). *Management and ideology: The legacy of the international scientific management movement.* Berkeley, CA: University of California Press.

Miller, M. C. (2005). Introduction. In Bernays, E. (1928/2005). *Propaganda.* Brooklyn: IG Publishing: 9–36.

Mirlees, T. (2016). *Hearts and mines: The US empire's culture industry.* Vancouver, BC: University of British Columbia Press.

Miskimmon, A., O'Loughlin, B. and Roselle, L. (2014). *Strategic narratives: Communication power and the new world order.* London: Routledge.

Monbiot, G. (2017). Frightened by Donald Trump? You don't know the half of it. *The Guardian*. Available online at: www.theguardian.com/commentisfree/2016/nov/30/donald-trump-george-monbiot-misinformation.

The Moving Picture World. (1918). *The moving picture world* (Vol. 33). New York, NY: Edward Warren.

Mullen, M. G. (2009, August 28). Strategic communication: Getting back to basics. *Foreign Policy*. Available online at: http://foreignpolicy.com/2009/08/28/strategic-communication-getting-back-to-basics/.

Muller, J. (2012, June 1). GM unloads $26 Billion in white-collar pensions: Could union workers be next? *Forbes*. Available online at: www.forbes.com/sites/joann muller/2012/06/01/gm-unloads-26-billion-in-white-collar-pensions-could-union-workers-be-next/#2c77e4862f07.

National Center for Education Statistics. (2016). *Literacy from 1870 to 1979*. Washington, DC. Available online at: https://nces.ed.gov/naal/lit_history.asp.

Neuzil, M. (1996). Hearst, Roosevelt, and the muckrake speech of 1906: A new perspective. *Journalism and Mass Communication Quarterly*, 73 (1): 29–39.

Newman, J. (2017, January 16). Bruce Springsteen cover band drops out of Trump inauguration party. *Rolling Stone*. Available online at: www.rollingstone.com/music/news/bruce-springsteen-cover-band-drops-out-of-donald-trump-party-w461203.

Newman, N., Fletcher, F., Levy, D.A.L. and Nielsen, R. K. (2016). *Reuters institute digital news report 2016*. Oxford: Reuters Institute for the Study of News.

OECD. (2016). Pension fund investments down slightly in 2015. In *Pension funds in figures, June 2016*. Paris: OECD. Available online at: www.oecd.org/daf/fin/private-pensions/Pension-funds-pre-data-2016.pdf.

Ogden, C. K. and Richards, I. A. (1923/1989), *The meaning of meaning*. Orlando, FL: Harcourt, Brace, and Janovich.

Oliver, K. (2009). *Command attention: Promoting your organization the Marine Corps way*. Annapolis, MD: Naval Institute Press.

Ong, W. J. (1977). *Interfaces of the word. Studies in the evolution of consciousness and culture*. Ithaca, NY: Cornell University Press.

Ong, W. J. (1971). *Rhetoric, romance, and technology: Studies in the interaction of expression and culture*. Ithaca, NY: Cornell University Press.

Osborne, S. (2016, December 12). Comey FBI letter 'almost certainly' cost Hillary Clinton the election, numbers reveal. *The Independent*. Available online at: www.independent.co.uk/news/world/americas/hillary-clinton-james-comey-fbi-letter-cost-election-a7468831.html.

Pacey, A. (1999/2001). *Meaning in technology*. Cambridge, MA: MIT Press.

Paddypower. (2017). *US Presidential election 2020*. Available online at: www.paddypower.com/bet/politics/other-politics/us-politics?ev_oc_grp_ids=2711243

Paltrow, S. J. (2013, November 18). Special report: The Pentagon's doctored ledgers conceal epic waste. *Reuters*. Available online at: www.reuters.com/article/us-usa-pentagon-waste-specialreport-idUSBRE9AH0LQ20131118.

Papadopoulou, M. and Babalioutas, D. (2007). Teaching critical literacy through print advertisements: An intervention with 6th grade students (Ages 11–12). *The International Journal of Learning*, *14*: 117–127.

Parker, J. (2016, March 15). General Motors' pension obligations and bad phase of bankruptcy. *Market Realist*. Available online at: http://marketrealist.com/2016/03/general-motors-pension-obligations-bad-phase-bankruptcy/

Peirce, C. S. (1905). What pragmatism is. *The Monist, 15* (2): 161–181.

Peirce, C. S. (1861). A treatise on metaphysics. In J. Hoopes (2014) (Ed.), *Peirce on signs: writings on semiotic*. Chapel Hill, NC: University of North Carolina Press.

Perez, S. (2016, November 10). Analysis of social media did a better job at predicting Trump's win than the polls. *Tech Crunch*. Available online at: https://techcrunch.com/2016/11/10/social-media-did-a-better-job-at-predicting-trumps-win-than-the-polls/

Peters, T. (1997). The brand called you: You can't move up if you don't stand out. *Fast Company*. Available online at: www.fastcompany.com/28905/brand-called-you. Accessed October 17, 2016.

Picketty, T. (2014). *Capital in the twenty-first century* (Trans. A. Goldhammer). Cambridge, MA: The Bleknap Press of Harvard University Press.

Pomerantsev, P. (2016). Why we're post-fact. *Granta*. Available online at: http://granta.com/why-were-post-fact/

Pomerantsev, P. (2014). The hidden author of Putinism. *The Atlantic*. Available online at: www.theatlantic.com/international/archive/2014/11/hidden-author-putinism-russia-vladislav-surkov/382489/.

Postman, N. (1985). *Amusing ourselves to death: Public discourse in the age of show business*. London: Penguin.

Pratt, S. L. (2002). *Native pragmatism: Rethinking the roots of American philosophy*. Bloomington, IN: Indiana University Press.

Ranney, A. (1976). "The divine science": Political engineering in American culture. *The American Political Science Review, 70* (1): 140–148.

Reagan, M. D. (1961). The business and defense services administration, 1953–57. *The Western Political Quarterly, 14* (2): 569–586.

Reich, R. (2017, January 7). Trump's tweedicts: The president-elect's tweets drive news, gain the power of implied threats. *Salon*. Available online at: www.salon.com/2017/01/08/trumps-tweedicts-the-president-elects-tweets-drive-news-gain-the-power-of-implied-threats_partner/.

Reitman, J. (1998). The Muckraker vs. the millionaire. *Scholastic Update, 131* (5): 14.

Reuters. (2016). Donald Trump piles Twitter pressure on Lockheed. *Reuters*. Available online at: http://fortune.com/2016/12/22/donald-trump-lockheed-f35-fighter-boeing-twitter/.

Richards, I. A. (1936). *The philosophy of rhetoric*. London: Oxford University Press.

Roberts, S. (2017, January 23). YouTuber promises to release sex tape. *News.com.au*. Available online at: www.news.com.au/lifestyle/real-life/news-life/youtuber-promises-to-release-sex-tape/news-story/e2140530c0fc7c7e6d31cecda89bbc39.

Robertson, A. (2016, October 17). Kremlin calls Joe Biden's threat to 'cyber strike' Russia 'unprecedented' and pledges to protect itself from the 'aggressive, unpredictable United States'. *Daily Mail*. Available online at: www.dailymail.co.uk/news/article-3839467/Are-ready-WAR-Russia-tells-civilians-check-bomb-shelters-gas-masks-nuclear-forces-advance-prepares-cyber-strike.html. Accessed October 17, 2016.

Robinson, P. (2016). Facebook vs. Twitter: Social media strategy differences. *Meltwater.* Available online at: www.meltwater.com/au/blog/facebook-vs-twitter-social-media-strategy-differences/

Rosselini, D. (2008). *Woodrow Wilson and the American myth in Italy culture, diplomacy, and war propaganda* (Trans. A. Shugaar). Boston, MA: Harvard University Press.

Russell, K. M. and Bishop, K. O. (2005). Understanding Ivy Lee's declaration of principles: U.S. newspaper and magazine coverage of publicity and press agentry, 1865–1904. *Public Relations Review, 35*: 91–101.

Sallet, J. (2015, September 25). Remarks of Jon Sallet, Federal Communications Commission General Counsel as prepared for delivery to the Telecommunications Policy Research Conference. *The Federal Communications Commission and Lessons of Recent Mergers & Acquisitions Reviews.* Available online at: https://apps.fcc.gov/edocs_public/attachmatch/DOC-335494A1.pdf

Schudson, M. (2008). The "Lippmann-Dewey Debate" and the Invention of Walter Lippmann as an Anti-Democrat 1985–1996. *International Journal of Communication, 2*: 1031–1042.

Scott, P. (2016, December 6). Lies, damned lies, statistics and university performance targets. *The Guardian.* Available online at: www.theguardian.com/education/2016/dec/06/lies-university-performance-targets-peter-scott.

Sengupta, K. (2017, January 16). Head of MI6 used information from Trump dossier in first public speech. *The Independent.* Available online at: www.independent.co.uk/news/world/americas/donald-trump-dossier-mi6-christopher-steele-russia-documents-alex-younger-a7528681.html.

Seyb, R. P. (2015). What Walter Saw: Walter Lippmann, The New York World, and scientific advocacy as an alternative to the News-Opinion dichotomy. *Journalism History, 41* (2): 58–72.

Shane, S. (2015, April 23). Drone strikes reveal uncomfortable truth: U.S. is often unsure about who will die. *New York Times.* Available online at: www.nytimes.com/2015/04/24/world/asia/drone-strikes-reveal-uncomfortable-truth-us-is-often-unsure-about-who-will-die.html.

Sharman, J. (2017, January 24). Sweden gang rape 'live-streamed on Facebook'. *The Independent.* Available online at: www.independent.co.uk/news/world/europe/sweden-uppsala-gang-rape-live-streamed-facebook-social-media-three-arrested-a7540176.html.

Shearer, D. R. (1996). *Industry, state, and society in Stalin's Russia, 1926–1934.* Cornell, NY: Cornell University Press.

Sills, J. (2008). Becoming your own brand. *Psychology Today.* Available online at: www.psychologytoday.com/articles/200801/becoming-your-own-brand.

Silverstein, K. (2000). Ford and the Führer. *The Nation.* Available online at: www.thenation.com/article/ford-and-fuhrer/.

Smith, A. (1776/1997). *The wealth of nations (Books I-III).* London: Penguin.

Smith, K. (2016, May 17). *Brandwatch.* Available online at: www.brandwatch.com/blog/44-twitter-stats-2016/.

Smythe, D. (1981). *Dependency road: Communication, consciousness, and Canada.* New York, NY: Ablex.

Snell, K. (2017, January 20). White House website touts Melania Trump's modeling and jewelry line. *The Washington Post.* Available online at: www.washingtonpost.com/news/powerpost/wp/2017/01/20/white-house-website-promotes-melania-trumps-modeling-and-jewelry-line/.

Sportsbet. (2017). *US Politics.* Available online at: www.sportsbet.com.au/betting/politics/us-politics.

Stephenson, C. (1943). Feudalism and its antecedents in England. *The American Historical Review, 48* (2): 245–265.

Stephenson, C. (1941). The origin and significance of feudalism. *The American Historical Review, 46* (4): 245–265.

Stott, P. (2016, May 31). How Government spending is affecting the consulting industry. *The Vault: Rankings and Reviews.* Available online at: www.vault.com/blog/consult-this-consulting-careers-news-and-views/how-government-spending-is-affecting-the-consulting-industry/.

Suchoff, B. (1972). Bartók and Serbo-Croatian folk music. *The Musical Quarterly, 58* (4): 557–571.

Swann, P. A. (2006). Got Web? Investing in a District website. *School Administrator, 63* (5): 24–31.

Swayne, J. (2017, January 23). Donald Trump's team defends 'alternative facts' after widespread protests. *The Guardian.* www.theguardian.com/us-news/2017/jan/22/donald-trump-kellyanne-conway-inauguration-alternative-facts.

Tarbell, I. M. (1902). *The history of the standard oil company* (Vol I and II). New York, NY: McLure, Phillips and Co. Available online at: www.pagetutor.com/standard/title1.html.

Tatham, S. (2013). *U.S. Governmental information operations and strategic communications: A discredited tool or user failure? Implications for future conflict.* Washington, DC: Global Security. Available online at: www.globalsecurity.org/military/library/report/2013/ssi_tatham.htm.

Taylor, F. W. (1911). *The principles of scientific management.* New York, NY: Harper and Brothers Publishers.

Taylor, P. M. (2003). *Munitions of the mind: A history of propaganda from the ancient world to the present era.* Manchester: Manchester University Press.

Thurow, L. C. (1996). *The future of capitalism: How today's economic forces will shape tomorrow's world.* St Leonards, Australia: Allen & Unwin.

Tumulty, K., Wagner, J. and O'Keefe, E. (2017, January 18). *Trump Cabinet nominees meet growing ethical questions.* Available online at: www.washingtonpost.com/politics/trump-cabinet-nominees-meet-growing-ethical-questions/2017/01/18/a7d82af8-ddaf-11e6-acdf-14da832ae861_story.html?hpid=hp_hp-top-table-main_nomineeproblems-855pm%3Ahomepage%2Fstory

US Department of Defense (DoD). (2017). *Contracts.* Washington, DC: US DoD. Available online at: www.defense.gov/News/Contracts

United States Congress. (2017). *H.R.193—American Sovereignty Restoration Act of 2017.* Washington, DC: US Congress. Available online at: www.congress.gov/bill/115th-congress/house-bill/193.

Vague, R. (2014, September 9). Government debt isn't the problem—private debt is. *The Atlantic*. Available online at: www.theatlantic.com/business/archive/2014/09/government-debt-isnt-the-problemprivate-debt-is/379865/.

Veblen, T. (1923). *Absentee ownership and business enterprise in recent times: The case of America*. New York, NY: B. W. Huebsch.

Veblen, T. (1906). The place of science in modern civilization. *American Journal of Sociology*, *11* (5): 585–609.

Walsh, K. T. (2009, January 16). Why too much inauguration star power could hurt Obama: A look at the past relationships between presidents and Hollywood. *US News*. Available online at: www.usnews.com/news/obama/articles/2009/01/16/why-too-much-inauguration-star-power-could-hurt-obama.

Watson, J. B. (1913/1994). Psychology as the behaviorist views it. *Psychological Review*, *2* (2): 48–253.

Weber, M. (1930/1992). *The protestant ethic and the spirit of capitalism*. London: Routledge.

Weinberg, A. and Weinberg, L. (1961/2001). Introduction. In A. Weinberg and L. Weinberg (1961/2001) (Eds.), *The muckrakers*. Chicago: University of Illinois Press: xvii–xxix.

Weinberg, S. (2008). *Taking on the trust: The epic battle of Ida Tarbell and John D. Rockefeller*. New York, NY: W.W. Norton.

White, L. T. (1962). *Medieval technology and social change*. London: Oxford University Press.

Whitman, J. Q. (1991). Of corporatism, fascism, and the first new deal. *The American Journal of Comparative Law*, *39* (4): 747–778.

Wilson, W. (1919). Remarks at the Philharmonic Club in Turin, Italy, January 6, 1919. *The American Presidency Project*. Available online at: www.presidency.ucsb.edu/ws/?pid=117765.

Wilson, W. (1917). *Address to a joint session of Congress requesting a declaration of war against Germany*. Available online at: www.presidency.ucsb.edu/ws/?pid=65366.

Wilson, W. (1916). Address to the salesmanship congress in Detroit, Michigan, July 10. *The American Presidency Project*. Available online at: www.presidency.ucsb.edu/ws/?pid=117701.

Wilson, W. (1887). Scientific administration. *Political Science Quarterly*, *2* (2): 197–222.

Wired. (2016). Why ISIS is winning the social media war. *Wired*. Available online at: www.wired.com/2016/03/isis-winning-social-media-war-heres-beat/.

Wodak, R. (2001). The discourse-historical approach. In R. Wodak and M. Meyers (Eds.), *Methods of critical discourse analysis*. London: Sage: 63–94.

Zephoria Digital Marketing. (2017). The top 20 valuable Facebook statistics—Updated January 2017. *Zephoria Digital Marketing*. Available online at: https://zephoria.com/top-15-valuable-facebook-statistics/.

Zipes, J. (2014). Introduction: Rediscovering the original tales of the brothers Grimm. In W. Grimm and J. Grimm (Eds.) (J. Zipes, trans.), *The original folk and fairy tales of the brothers Grimm: The complete first edition*. Princeton, NJ: Princeton University Press.

Multimedia Links

1920s television. Available online at: www.youtube.com/watch?v=OO2g0AzLy6I

Birth of a nation. (Griffith, 1915). Available online at: www.youtube.com/watch?v=vZ871wZd7UY).

Cleopatra. (Fox, 1917). Available online at: www.youtube.com/watch?v=KfFYU7G7eEM)

Creel committee poster images. (2016). Available online at: www.google.com.au/search?q=creel+committee+posters&espv=2&biw=1900&bih=916&tbm=isch&tbo=u&source=univ&sa=X&ved=0ahUKEwj7nfSwuObQAhXHJJQKHa5PB6UQsAQIHw#imgrc=sKezmmvcg6DqQM%3A

Idiocracy. (2006). *President Camacho speech*. Available online at: https://vimeo.com/82074066

Intolerance. (Griffith, 1916). Available online at: www.youtube.com/watch?v=eo66cJqEl4A)

Index

administration 2, 65, 71
advertising 3–9, 17, 22–3, 35,
    43–7, 53–4, 62–3, 84, 87–92,
    100, 104
art 19, 39, 51, 62–3, 90–1
Auerbach, Jonathan 11, 35, 37, 47–8,
    50–1, 54–5, 60, 63, 90

bankers 69, 97
behaviourism 22, 57
Bentham, Jeremy 30, 50, 103
billboard 39
Blumer, Herbert 50
brand 7–8, 12, 53, 93, 96–7,
    100–1, 105
Brexit 3, 13
broadcast 3, 12, 69, 107
Burke, Kenneth 3–5, 8–10, 12, 19–20,
    27–31, 34–5, 48–9, 75, 84, 89,
    91–2, 105

campaign 1, 34, 43–4, 50, 54, 63,
    83–4, 87, 100
Charlemagne 67
comitatus 11, 64, 67, 69–70, 72, 80
committee 1–2, 11, 67, 71, 121
communication 1–9, 11–13, 27, 35,
    44–5, 47–50, 55–8, 60–2, 75,
    79–80, 83, 85, 91, 94–5, 99–104,
    111–15
community 15, 37–8, 53, 86,
    90, 107
content analysis 55
context 2, 5, 9, 33–4, 39, 50–1, 71, 73,
    92, 98
corporatism 65–78, 96
cosmopolitan 17, 36, 109

cosmopolitanism 96
CPI 1–12, 14, 17, 27–59, 64–5, 73,
    77–9, 86, 89–90, 95, 106
Creel, George 1–14, 17, 27–48, 51–3,
    62, 64, 74, 96, 98, 102, 106
crisis 2, 12, 35, 51, 67–8, 72, 74, 76,
    79, 91, 96, 104
critical 4, 10, 48–9, 51, 62, 91–2, 96,
    98, 101, 106
culture 7, 14, 18, 23, 25–6, 30, 35, 41,
    45, 58–9, 62, 94, 96

debt 68–9, 74–7, 111, 119
democracy 18, 99, 111
Dewey, John 2, 32–3, 90, 96, 98,
    111, 114
dialectic 47, 103, 106
discourse 3–4, 8, 10, 27, 36, 64, 96
dramatism 32, 87
dramatistic 3–5, 7, 22, 32, 90

ecosystem 13
education 18–23, 39, 53–4, 70–1, 91,
    103–6, 111–18
Entertainer-In-Chief 85
entertainment 9, 11, 73, 79–81, 83,
    87–8, 98
entertainmentisation 11, 81–9
ethics 3–4, 13, 20, 52, 82, 85

Facebook 84, 87, 97, 100
facts 3–11, 17, 20–8, 30–7, 39,
    44, 46, 51, 55–61, 64, 70, 72,
    76, 78, 83, 86–90, 94, 98–9,
    102–3, 106
fascism 60
Four Minute Men 37

gender 15, 91
globalisation 3, 77, 96
grammar 17

Halliday, Michael 4
hate 46
Hitler, Adolf 55, 59–63
Hollywood 40, 43, 84

ideals 2, 30, 46, 55
ignorance 46, 49
indebtedness 73, 75–6
internet 3, 11, 55, 57, 83, 87–8, 95,
    97–8

James, William 1, 4, 26–7, 31–3, 39,
    48, 59, 86, 94
Jansen, Sue Curry 11, 48–52,
    90, 98
journalism 16–17, 20, 23, 50,
    53, 67
journalists 1, 7, 90, 97–8
justice 16, 45

language 3
Leviathan 52
liberty 45–6
lies 9, 32, 46, 88, 90, 105
linguistics 4–5, 8, 47, 50, 103, 106
Lippmann, Walter 11, 30, 34,
    48–52, 60, 86, 90, 96, 98,
    105–6
literacy 2, 10, 58–9, 62, 91, 96
logological 19–20

Malinowski, Bronislaw 4–5, 8,
    103, 115
management 6, 20–3, 27, 56–7, 61–2,
    73, 97, 101
marketing 2–3, 17, 35, 63, 114
media 1–10, 12, 17, 35, 37, 54–6,
    62–3, 69, 73, 79, 83–7, 92,
    97–100, 105
Merton, Robert K. 50, 52
militarisation 4, 12, 75, 77, 79, 102
militarism 2, 12, 77
military 1, 6, 9–15, 23, 40–3,
    46, 60, 66–9, 71–9, 84–8, 94,
    98–102
moral 13, 20–1, 30, 41, 43, 50–1,
    71–3, 75–7, 87, 91, 99–104

muckrake 2, 16–17, 20, 28, 36, 51
multimedia 39, 93

nationalism 3, 9, 47, 60, 77, 82,
    84, 96
neofeudal corporatism 2, 8, 11–12, 35,
    65–7, 72, 75–8, 85
news 12, 17, 30–1, 35–7, 42, 44,
    50–4, 64, 74–5, 81–91, 94, 97–9

Ong, Walter 4, 9, 20, 29, 35, 116

Paramount 40
parasitism 54, 89–93
Park, Robert 50
Peirce, C. S. 27, 31–3, 50, 116
persuasion 5–6, 18, 29–30,
    40, 101
philosophy 10, 27, 32, 49–50, 54,
    95, 117
pietistic 91
piety 91–3, 98
Plato 60, 103, 113
Pomerantsev, Peter 4, 63–4,
    102, 117
posters 1, 39, 121
post-fact 4, 86, 117
pragmatic 4, 21–7, 31–6, 74, 91, 95
pragmatism 8, 19–27, 31, 33, 46,
    50, 56
privatisation 50, 65, 68
propaganda 3–4, 10, 30, 35, 47–8,
    50–8, 62–3, 73, 90, 102
proposals 4, 33
propositions 4
psychology 20, 22
public relations 6–7, 9, 63
purpose 12, 19–20, 25–7, 32–4, 46,
    48, 64, 82, 99, 101

radio 3, 48, 54–5, 58–60, 80, 86, 95,
    111, 114
reform 15–16, 28
rhetoric 3–10, 13, 17–20, 27–40, 43,
    46–9, 51, 56, 64–9, 72, 77, 82–92,
    95–6, 103–7
romanticism 10, 41
Russia 7, 50, 55, 61–4, 85, 96, 101–2

Santayana, George 50
Sarbanes-Oxley act 72, 108

science 14, 23–5, 87, 106
scientism 21, 23, 26, 28, 31–2, 57, 87, 90, 103
Smith-Mundt act 3
statistics 84, 87–8
stereotypes 34, 49–50, 105
strategy 43, 48, 57, 62, 79, 83–4, 100–2, 104–5
stupid 22, 43
Surkov, Vladislav 63–4, 101–2, 105

Taliban 104
technologies 3, 9, 19–20, 54, 62, 80, 83
tools 19–20, 99, 102
transparency 46, 57, 61, 90
Trump, Donald 3–4, 13, 72, 77, 80, 82–8, 92–5, 98, 105–6, 108–19

truth 4, 13, 23, 26–7, 29, 31–3, 46, 60, 87, 90–1, 93, 105, 109, 118
Twitter 80–3, 85, 93–4, 97–8, 117–18

universal 38, 40, 67
usenet 97

Veblen, T. 23–30, 70–3, 119–20
verisimilitude 31–2
Vietnam 63, 74, 92, 95, 98, 104

Wilson, Woodrow 1–19, 45–7, 51, 55–6, 73–4, 95–6
Wodak, Ruth 3
words 3

YouTube 7, 97–9

For Product Safety Concerns and Information please contact our EU
representative GPSR@taylorandfrancis.com Taylor & Francis Verlag GmbH,
Kaufingerstraße 24, 80331 München, Germany

Printed and bound by CPI Group (UK) Ltd, Croydon, CR0 4YY
11/04/2025
01844009-0015